D0911942

"I welcome this practical resource that clearly helps to provide authoritative advice on this key subject. Mental health and wellbeing are important, and too often ignored, it is great to see clear explanation and practical advice in this comprehensive text."

Dr Steven Boorman CBE, Director of Employee Health

"This book is a valuable resource in helping us meet the challenge of recognising mental health issues in the workplace. As a society, we're gradually chipping away at the stigma that still exists, and through Gill and Donna's work on this book and the work pioneered at Brighton and Sussex University Hospitals, we can continue to change attitudes and promote genuine wellbeing at work."

Dame Marianne Griffiths, Chief Executive
of Western Sussex Hospitals NHS Foundation Trust

"This is a valuable resource, especially for employers, managers and employees but also for all concerned about mental health at work. It tackles some of the most important challenges in today's workplace, and makes good use of recent evidence."

Professor Dame Carol Black, Expert Advisor
on Health and Work to the Department
of Health and Public Health England

Mental Health and Wellbeing in the Workplace is a must-have book for both employees and employers.

Beautifully written, easy to follow and packed with vital knowledge and practical strategies. This is not an opinion-based book. Its' evidence based, referencing fascinating studies because the expert authors have really done their homework and brought this together with their wealth of actual experience on the subject. With the ever-growing crisis of stress related illness in the workplace and mental health problems in society at large, these experts have given readers a true gift in knowing how to properly support self- care and for employers, the caring of others.

Dr Margot Sunderland, D.Psych - Director and Founder of The Institute for Arts in Therapy and Education

Mental Health
and Wellbeing
in the Workplace

Mental Health and Wellbeing in the Workplace

A Practical Guide for Employers and Employees

Gill Hasson

Donna Butler

CAPSTONE
A Wiley Brand

This edition first published 2020
© 2020 Gill Hasson & Donna Butler.

Registered office
John Wiley & Sons Ltd, The Atrium, Southern Gate, Chichester, West Sussex, PO19
8SQ, United Kingdom

For details of our global editorial offices, for customer services and for information
about how to apply for permission to reuse the copyright material in this book please see
our website at www.wiley.com.

All rights reserved. No part of this publication may be reproduced, stored in a retrieval
system, or transmitted, in any form or by any means, electronic, mechanical,
photocopying, recording or otherwise, except as permitted by the UK Copyright, Designs
and Patents Act 1988, without the prior permission of the publisher.

Wiley publishes in a variety of print and electronic formats and by print-on-demand.
Some material included with standard print versions of this book may not be included in
e-books or in print-on-demand. If this book refers to media such as a CD or DVD that is
not included in the version you purchased, you may download this material at http://
booksupport.wiley.com. For more information about Wiley products, visit www.wiley
.com.

Designations used by companies to distinguish their products are often claimed as
trademarks. All brand names and product names used in this book are trade names,
service marks, trademarks or registered trademarks of their respective owners. The
publisher is not associated with any product or vendor mentioned in this book.

Limit of Liability/Disclaimer of Warranty: While the publisher and author have used
their best efforts in preparing this book, they make no representations or warranties with
respect to the accuracy or completeness of the contents of this book and specifically
disclaim any implied warranties of merchantability or fitness for a particular purpose. It
is sold on the understanding that the publisher is not engaged in rendering professional
services and neither the publisher nor the author shall be liable for damages arising
herefrom. If professional advice or other expert assistance is required, the services of a
competent professional should be sought.

Library of Congress Cataloging-in-Publication Data

Names: Hasson, Gill, author. | Butler, Donna (Donna Margaret), author.
Title: Mental health and wellbeing in the workplace : a practical guide for
   employers and employees / Gill Hasson, Donna Butler.
Description: Chichester, West Sussex : Wiley-Capstone, 2020. | Includes
   bibliographical references and index.
Identifiers: LCCN 2020004334 (print) | LCCN 2020004335 (ebook) | ISBN
   9780857088284 (paperback) | ISBN 9780857088307 (adobe pdf) | ISBN
   9780857088291 (epub)
Subjects: LCSH: Psychology, Industrial—Great Britain. | Employees—Mental
   health—Great Britain. | Quality of work life—Great Britain. | Employee
   health promotion—Great Britain. | Personnel management—Great Britain.
   | Work—Psychological aspects. | Work environment—Psychological
   aspects.
Classification: LCC HF5548.8 .H353 2020 (print) | LCC HF5548.8 (ebook) |
   DDC 158.7—dc23
LC record available at https://lccn.loc.gov/2020004334
LC ebook record available at https://lccn.loc.gov/2020004335

Cover Design: Wiley
Cover Image: © Elaine Barker/Shutterstock

Set in 12/15pt, SabonLTStd by SPi Gobal, Chennai, India

Printed in Great Britain by TJ International Ltd, Padstow, Cornwall, UK

10 9 8 7 6 5 4 3 2 1

Contents

To our sons Jake and Tom who brought us together.

Foreword

A dults in employment spend a large proportion of their time at work, so our jobs and workplaces can have a big impact on our physical and mental health and wellbeing. There is clear evidence that good work improves health and wellbeing across people's lives, both in terms of quality of life and economically. This entails working in an environment that is safe, as well as having a sense of security, autonomy, control, good line management and good communication.

However, for some people, work can also be a cause of stress and anxiety and alongside life's challenges, people's circumstances and experiences can further compound problems, which can lead to experiencing common mental health problems. This puts further strain on individuals and those they care for and about.

There is a growing emphasis amongst politicians, academics, trade unions, mental health organisations, employers large and small and workers on promoting good mental health and preventing mental ill health. This is important, as one in four adults experiences at least one mental health problem in any given year, and early signs of poor mental health, including feeling anxious, stressed, having low mood or trouble sleeping, can affect everyone. And in 2018, 17.5million working days were lost in the UK due to stress, depression, anxiety and serious mental health problem-related sickness absence. This costs UK employers an estimated £8 billion per year in lost productivity.

Supporting good mental health is about having a whole workplace approach as part of overall health and wellbeing, preventing problems, and intervening early and providing effective support and care to those experiencing mental illnesses. It is also about working in a way that encourages and supports good practice amongst managers and staff alike, and having a compassionate environment that values everyone.

At Public Health England, we have established better mental health as one of our ten priorities in our 2020-2025 strategy. Our aim is to ensure that mental health has parity with physical health, modelling the role that organisations can play as employers whilst embedding good mental health across our own work. We are also supporting the NHS on the mental health components of their Long Term Plan, including suicide prevention and new models of care to improve the health and wellbeing of people with severe mental illness.

This book provides resources to empower employers and their staff to plan ahead for the near and long-term future, on everything to do with promoting good mental health in the workplace. It highlights a variety of practical steps that can be taken intertwined with stories and case studies. The themes that run throughout are the importance of open, supportive communication and of training and education for employers, management and staff.

Wellbeing and good mental health are not only good for the individual and their ability to thrive and enjoy their work, but it is also vital for the prosperity and productivity of their organisation, a veritable win:win for everyone.

Duncan Selbie
Chief Executive of Public Health England

Introduction

How we spend our days is, of course, how we spend our lives.

Annie Dillard

For many of us, a large part of our days is spent at work; it's reckoned that we will spend 3507 days at work over a lifetime. The average person spends a quarter of their adult life at work. Work can give us a sense of purpose, structure, and satisfaction while also providing the means to finance daily life. It can also cause stress.

In fact, mental health and wellbeing at work is one of the most important issues facing all of us. Global organizations, national organizations, small organizations, trade unions, politicians, mental health organizations, employers, and, of course, employees, their families and friends are all becoming increasingly concerned about mental health and wellbeing in the workplace.

Managing mental health and wellbeing at work starts with understanding what mental health and wellbeing are. In Chapter 1 we explain this. We also explain what mental ill-health is and we describe the signs and symptoms of some common mental illnesses. Our mental health and wellbeing can change not just from day to day, month to month, and year to year, but at key stages and changes in our lives; you'll also read in Chapter 1 how some key life stages can adversely impact on our mental health and wellbeing.

In Chapter 2 we look at the impact that work can have on our mental health and wellbeing. We ask the question 'Is work good for you?' The answer is yes. And no. The research consistently reflects what we all already know: people are suffering at work; they're finding the increasing demands of work pressure untenable.

Issues such as a poor working environment, unrealistic deadlines, poor communication, poor interpersonal relationships, too much responsibility, and a lack of management support can significantly impact on the wellbeing of people at work. People get stressed. Especially if they're also dealing with difficulties and problems outside of work. People get stressed when they feel overwhelmed or unable to cope as a result of pressures and demands that are unmanageable; when they feel they have little control over a situation.

It doesn't have to be this way! In recent years, there's been plenty of interest and research telling us how to turn things around. In 2017, for example, an independent review – *Thriving at Work* – led by mental health campaigner Lord Dennis Stevenson and Paul Farmer, chief executive at Mind and chair of the NHS Mental Health Taskforce. *Thriving at Work* sets out a framework of core standards that all UK employers, it suggests – no matter what their size or the industry in which they operate – can implement to address workplace wellbeing and mental health.

In Chapter 3 we explain how organizations and managers at all levels can implement some of the recommendations made in the *Thriving at Work* review. You'll read how to assess, improve, and maintain wellbeing in the workplace. In other words, how to be a good place to work.

Of course, it's not all down to organizations and their leaders to up their game. There's a lot that individual employees can do to develop their own wellbeing and resilience. Chapter 4 has a wealth of practical advice and suggestions that can help individuals to, amongst other things, have a healthy work–life balance, manage stress at work, create positive relationships with colleagues, and look after their physical health at work.

However, although there's plenty that each of us can do to develop and maintain our wellbeing, we're not invincible. For one reason or another, any of us can experience a mental illness. In Chapter 5 we look at how best to manage at work if you have been or are currently unwell. We explain the importance of identifying what could trigger a downturn, what you can do to help yourself to be well, and what to do in a crisis. Throughout this chapter and the previous one, we emphasize the importance of not needing to do any of this – looking after your mental health and wellbeing – on your own. There *is* help and support out there.

In the last chapter – Chapter 6 – we write about how managers can help and support employees with mental health problems. There's a lot to take into account, but if you are a manager, do be reassured that no one is expecting you to know all the answers, or to know as much as a trained mental health professional. But having some knowledge, understanding, and training in mental health *will* help you know when and how far you can help, when to ask for support, and when to refer someone to other agencies.

Employers that genuinely promote and value wellbeing and good mental health and support people – whatever their culture, beliefs, and abilities – with mental health problems are more likely to create conditions that allow for everyone to give of their best, to be committed to their organization's goals and values, to be motivated to contribute to organizational success, to feel valued and supported, and to have a positive sense of their own wellbeing.

1
Understanding Mental Health and Wellbeing

Defining Mental Health and Wellbeing

The World Health Organization (WHO) defines mental health as: 'A state of well-being in which every individual realizes his or her own potential, can cope with the normal stresses of life, can work productively and fruitfully and is able to make a contribution to her or his community'.

Our mental health affects the way we experience the world; how we think, feel, and behave towards ourselves and others. WHO defines mental health as a 'state of well-being' and just as physical health is intrinsic to wellbeing, so is mental health.

The mental health organization 'Mind' suggests that if you have good mental wellbeing you are able to:

- feel relatively confident in yourself and have positive self-esteem
- feel and express a range of emotions
- build and maintain good relationships with others

- feel engaged with the world around you
- live and work productively
- deal with the stresses of daily life
- adapt and manage in times of change and uncertainty.

Both Mind and the World Health Organization's definition of mental health refer to a person's wellbeing. But is wellbeing the same as wellness?

When you think about wellness, think prevention and health. When you think about well-being, think happiness.

Susie Ellis. Chair of the Global Wellbeing Institute

Certainly, happiness is important, but there is more to wellbeing than the positive feelings that come with happiness. Both WHO and Mind recognize that wellbeing involves not just happiness, but crucially, the ability to manage difficulties, problems, and challenges; the 'normal stresses'.

In 2012, Cardiff Metropolitan University Professors Rachel Dodge and Annette P. Daly et al. published their report *The Challenge of Defining Wellbeing*. Having reviewed and analyzed past attempts by other researchers to define wellbeing, they concluded that 'it would be appropriate for a definition of wellbeing to centre on a state of equilibrium or balance that can be affected by life events or challenges'. Consequently they define wellbeing as: 'the balance point between an individual's resource pool and the challenges faced'.

In other words, wellbeing occurs when a person is able to enjoy life **and** has the resources to draw on to manage life's ups and downs without feeling overly stressed. Therefore, an important component of wellbeing is resilience; the ability to cope with, as well as bounce back and recover from, difficulties and challenges.

Dimensions of Wellbeing; Social and Spiritual

There is no health without mental health.

World Health Organization

One of the key aspects of mental wellbeing is our social wellbeing; the ability to build and maintain good relationships with others. Social wellbeing is the extent to which you feel a sense of belonging and social inclusion. The UK Faculty of Public Health suggests that social wellbeing is 'the basis for social equality and the antidote to issues such as racism, stigma, violence and crime' and that it is dependent on, amongst other things, 'the norm with regard to interpersonal relationships in a group, community or society, including respect for others and their needs, compassion and empathy, and authentic interaction'.

Another feature of wellbeing – just as important as social, mental, and emotional wellbeing, but not so widely acknowledged – is spiritual wellbeing. Spirituality refers to a sense of being connected to something bigger and more everlasting than yourself.

Spiritual wellbeing means the ability to experience and integrate meaning and purpose in life through a person's connectedness with self, others, art, music, literature, nature, or a power greater than oneself.

Spiritual wellbeing is about our inner life and its relationship with the wider world . . . Spiritual wellbeing does not just reflect religious belief although for people of a religious faith it is obviously a central feature.

Dr Ritika Srivastava

Physical and Mental Health and Wellbeing

Distinctions are often made between mind and body but when it comes to mental health and wellbeing and physical health and wellbeing, we can't think of them as separate entities. Poor physical health can lead to a person developing mental health problems. And poor mental health can have a negative impact on our physical health and wellbeing.

A physical health problem can impact on our cognitive and emotional abilities; adversely affecting our daily lives, our work, and our relationships. Conversely, if our mental health is suffering as a result of, for example, stress, depression, or anxiety, we are less likely to eat and sleep well and may be less physically active which, in turn, can impact our immune system and so our ability to resist infections and illness can be depleted.

Just as when we neglect and ignore our physical health we can become physically unwell, it's also the case that if we ignore or suppress difficult feelings we can become physically unwell.

When we are exposed to stressful experiences or trauma, we can, without realizing it, banish the experience to the unconscious; it's too much to deal with and it's pushed down to the basement of our minds. Eventually – sometimes years later – the stressful/traumatic experience can present as a mental health problem, for example an anxiety disorder. But a stressful or traumatic experience can also manifest itself as a physical disorder.

Case Study

One evening, Catrice was reversing her car into into the garage, when she heard a scream. She had reversed the car over her partner, Julie. Unknown to Catrice, Julie was sitting on the floor at the back of the garage, fixing her bike. Horrified and shocked, Catrice called an ambulance and Julie was taken to hospital. Although she had sustained serious injuries, they were not life threatening and in time, Julie recovered. However, a week after Julie's admission to hospital, Catrice developed a weakness in her lower limbs. Eventually she found that she was unable to stand; each time she tried, her legs gave way from underneath her.

Following weeks of tests, x-rays, physiotherapy assessments, and orthopaedic referral, Catrice's GP, believing that she was experiencing a 'somatic response' – a physical response to an emotional trauma – referred her to a psychotherapist.

Catrice had blocked the feelings – the trauma, stress, and guilt – she experienced as a result of Julie's suffering but those blocked feelings had manifested themselves as physical symptoms. With support from a psychotherapist, Catrice recovered; she was able to forgive herself for the pain and suffering Julie had been through as a result of her actions.

People with mental health problems are more likely to develop physical health problems and vice versa. Furthermore, people with mental health problems can present to their GP or employer complaining of physical symptoms that have no physical cause. This can sometimes lead to missed or delayed detection of the underlying mental health problem. The interaction between physical and mental health is complex and it is often difficult to determine the direction of causal relationships.

Professor Dame Carol Black

In the same way that the repression of stressful experiences can become a physical problem, physical health can impact on our mental health.

Psoriasis – an auto-immune condition affecting a person's skin – is an example of a condition which can impact on mental as well as physical wellbeing. A 2010 study published in the journal *Archives of Dermatology* found that those living with psoriasis are a third more likely than people without the disease to be depressed or anxious. The physical and psychological impacts can be cyclically linked: the condition can cause emotional distress which can trigger a psoriasis flare and, as a result, cause further distress.

Wellbeing is Subjective

A myriad of factors influence health and well-being, though many are familiar only to those who experience them.

Professor Dame Carol Black

Although there are key aspects to wellbeing – physical, mental and emotional, social and spiritual – wellbeing *is* subjective; each and every one of us has our own individual thoughts and beliefs about what makes for wellbeing. Our thoughts, ideas, beliefs, and experiences are framed in a narrative – we each have our own story – our own explanation or account of our wellbeing and what may or may not influence it.

For example, one person's account of their experience of depression and anxiety – how they feel, how they manage, and the extent of the impact on their wellbeing – will be different from someone else's experience and account. In another example, a person who is physically unwell or has a physical disability may feel that they have good levels of wellbeing *despite* illness or disability. Conversely, someone who is perceived as being well and 'able bodied' may believe and feel that they are *not* experiencing wellbeing to any great extent.

And, when it comes to traumatic experiences, professor of psychiatry at the University of North Carolina, Stephen Porges, suggests that the focus cannot be on the event, but on the individual reaction or response. 'Much of our society defines trauma by the event when the real critical issue is the individual's reaction. By not accepting that, we end up saying: "If I can survive this and do well, why can't you?" So we start blaming the survivors again.' Porges says that whatever the size or the intensity of the traumatic event 'when a person has a reaction or response to trauma, the body interprets the traumatic event as a life threat'.

Who Experiences Mental Ill-health and What Are the Causes?

'One in four' is widely cited as the number of people who suffer from a mental health problem. The Health Survey for England found in 2014 that one in four people reported having been diagnosed with at least one mental illness at some point in their lives. A further 18% said they'd experienced an illness but hadn't been diagnosed.

As with so much of what it means to be human, our levels of mental health and wellbeing are a result of both genetic (nature) and environmental factors (nurture).

Although no specific genes for depression have been identified, research has shown that if you have a close family member with depression, you are more likely to experience depression yourself. While this might be caused by our biology, (nature) this link could also be because we usually learn behaviour and ways of coping from the people around us as we grow up. (Nurture)

Mind

Many factors can contribute to the onset of a mental illness. These include prenatal stress, adverse childhood experiences (ACE), including childhood neglect, abuse, and trauma; stress; bereavement; relationship break-down; physical and sexual abuse; experiencing stigma or discrimination; unemployment; social isolation and loneliness; poverty, debt, homelessness or poor housing; physical illness or disability.

Mental ill-health can affect anyone, regardless of gender, age, race, ethnicity, religion, geography, sexual orientation, or other aspects of cultural background or identity. But some people are more vulnerable than others.

For example, 7.7 million adults aged 55+ say they have experienced depression and 7.3 million have suffered with anxiety, according to 2017 YouGov research for the charity Age UK. For people over 55, the death of loved ones, their own ill-health, and financial worries are the most common triggers for mental health problems.

In their 2016 report *Mental Health Problems in People with Learning Disabilities*, The National Institute for Health and Care Excellence (NICE) state that mental health problems in people with learning disabilities are more common than in the general population, with a point prevalence of about 30%.

People from a Black, Asian, and minority ethnic (BAME) background are, according to the UK Mental Health Foundation, generally at higher risk of mental ill-health. They also report that Post Traumatic Stress Disorder (PTSD) is more common in women of black ethnic origin.

The Mental Health Foundation report that evidence suggests people identifying as LGBT are at higher risk of experiencing poor mental health such as depression, suicidal thoughts, self-harm, and alcohol and substance misuse – compared to heterosexual people, due to a range of factors, including discrimination, isolation, and homophobia.

Whoever we are, whatever our circumstances, and whatever the statistics, what's most important is to recognize that we *all* have mental health. The spectrum ranges from a positive, healthy state to a poor or extremely poor state of mental health with severe symptoms or conditions. It's also important to know that our mental health can fluctuate, depending on life situations, and on how we manage our mental health.

Defining Mental Ill-health

Mental illness happens when the way a person thinks and behaves causes significant distress or impairs their ability to function. Mental disorders are usually defined by a combination of how a person thinks, feels, perceives and behaves.

The WHO state that 'Mental disorders comprise a broad range of problems, with different symptoms. However, they are generally characterized by some combination of abnormal thoughts, emotions, behaviour and relationships with others.'

Mental ill-health can develop gradually or be a sudden change in the way you approach your life and the way you think, feel, or react and this can create difficulties in your daily living. As a result, life can become very difficult to cope with. There can be periods where it is transitory, where the feelings, thoughts, and behaviours are not experienced for very long, or are intermittent. At other times it may be a prolonged and protracted episode, and seem as if it will never pass.

Mental health problems can range from problems such as depression and anxiety, eating disorders, and addictive behaviours, to rarer problems such as schizophrenia and bipolar disorder, personality disorders, and PTSD.

On their website, Mind explain that 'we all have times when we struggle with our mental health, but when these difficult experiences or feelings go on for a long time and affect our ability to enjoy and live our lives in the way we want to, this is a mental health problem. You might receive a specific diagnosis from your doctor, or just feel more generally that you are experiencing poor mental health.'

Recognizing and Understanding Specific Mental Health Problems

Stigma and lack of awareness surrounding the spectrum of mental health problems can mean that people are often not aware of the symptoms of even some of the most common disorders like depression and anxiety. A person can be struggling but they, their friends, family, colleagues etc. may not recognize that they have a mental health problem. This can mean the issue doesn't get talked about, support and treatment are not sought, and things can go from bad to worse.

Of course, just as one person can experience a physical health problem differently from the next person, one person can experience a mental health problem differently from someone else with a mental health problem. There are, however, some common signs and symptoms. They include any number of the following:

- Out-of-character behaviour/unusual reactions
- Being overly sensitive, often upset or tearful, perhaps unable to stop crying
- Sudden mood changes
- Aggressive behaviour, irrational, angry outbursts
- Withdrawing from others
- Persistent tiredness or exhaustion
- Sleep problems
- Difficulty communicating, thinking clearly, concentrating, remembering, or making decisions
- Changes in appetite and eating habits
- Using alcohol or drugs as a coping strategy
- Losing interest in sex or being dependent on it
- Neglecting appearance and personal hygiene
- Taking less interest in things that used to be enjoyable
- Reluctance to make plans
- Physical aches and pains, nausea, tremors
- Self-harm, suicidal thinking or behaviour.

Although these are common indicators of a mental health problem (and/or could also be symptoms of a physical illness) each mental health problem will have its own specific signs and symptoms.

Stress

Stress isn't a psychiatric diagnosis, but, say the mental health charity Mind, 'it's closely linked to your mental health in two important ways:

- Stress can cause mental health problems, and make existing problems worse. For example, if you often struggle to manage feelings of stress, you might develop a mental health problem like anxiety or depression.
- Mental health problems can cause stress. You might find coping with the day-to-day symptoms of your mental health problem, as well as potentially needing to manage medication, healthcare appointments or treatments, can become extra sources of stress.

This can start to feel like a vicious circle, and it might be hard to see where stress ends and your mental health problem begins.'

Emotional and physical responses:
- Overwhelmed, worried
- A sense of dread
- Racing thoughts that won't switch off
- Unable to concentrate, indecisive
- Being wound up, irritable, impatient, aggressive
- Muscle tension
- Headaches
- Chest pains
- Indigestion or heartburn

- Constipation or diarrhoea
- Feeling sick, dizzy, or faint.

How you might behave:

- Avoiding situations that are overwhelming you
- Being tearful, snapping at people
- Being unable to sit still
- Eating more or less than usual
- Smoking, drinking, or taking drugs 'to cope'
- Sleep problems.

Stress can lead to either or both of the two most common mental health problems: anxiety and depression.

Depression

Depression is a low mood that lasts for a long time and affects your everyday life. In its mildest form, depression can mean feeling sad, lacking enthusiasm, feeling that you have little control and being generally in low spirits.

We all feel down or sad at times. Sadness is the normal reaction caused by a loss or failure that we experience. When you lose something or someone you love, when you fail to achieve something – your hopes fail to materialize, or a good situation comes to an end – this experience of loss can be felt and expressed as sadness.

Depression doesn't necessarily stop you leading your normal life but it does make everything harder to do – to function well at work, to focus on tasks and complete them, for example – and outside of work, feeling depressed makes things seem less worthwhile. At its most severe, depression can result in feelings of despair and worthlessness and that you have no control over situations. It can lead to thoughts of harming oneself or others, or can lead to feeling suicidal.

Some common signs of depression may include:

Emotional and physical responses:
- Feeling restless, agitated, or irritable
- Feelings of guilt and worthlessness
- Little self-confidence or self-esteem
- Feeling down; a flat mood that doesn't shift; apathetic; empty and numb
- Feeling detached; a sense of unreality
- Little or no pleasure in life or things. Unable to see fun or humour in any situation
- Unable to relate to other people, feeling isolated from them
- Finding no pleasure in life or things you used to enjoy
- Not looking forward to anything or planning anything
- Feelings of hopelessness and despair.

How you might behave:
- Distancing yourself from family and friends
- Avoiding social events and activities you used to enjoy
- Moving slowly or, unable to rest, always on the move.

Anxiety

Anxiety is the anticipation of trouble, misfortune or adversity, difficulties or disaster. Anyone can feel stressed and anxious from time to time; to feel fearful at the thought of, for example, an upcoming medical test, a presentation at work, a job interview, or an exam. It is a normal response to a stressful, or perceived stressful, situation. Whatever it is that you may be anxious about, you may feel that you've no control over what could happen; how events might turn out and how you'll cope if things do go wrong.

But, like all emotions, anxiety can have a positive effect; it serves as your internal alarm and prompts you to take necessary measures to prevent the worst case scenario from happening. Most of the time, once the stressful situation is over, anxious feelings subside. There are, though, times when feelings of anxiety are more permanent and entrenched and adversely affect your mental health. Being anxious about how to cope can lead to being depressed because you feel you have little or no control over what's happening.

Just as the symptoms of depression will vary from person to person, so will the symptoms of anxiety. Anxiety may be experienced in some of the following ways:

Emotional and physical responses:
- Racing thoughts
- Fretting and ruminating

- Being jumpy and on edge, feeling 'wired', tense, irritable, impatient, angry
- Distrusting of and/or aggressive with others
- Irrational fears
- Feelings of impending doom
- Sensations of nausea, choking, or being unable to breathe or hyperventilating
- Feeling panicky; pounding heart/increased heart rate, chest pain (sweating/muscle tension/shaky)
- Fear of losing control
- IBS, headaches, migraines.

How you might behave:

- Becoming agitated, speedy; inability to rest
- Seeking constant approval or reassurance
- Needing to avoid or escape certain situations – social gatherings, for example, or being at work – any situation perceived as a threat
- Obsessive and controlling behaviour
- Taking a long time to calm down following upsets.

Burnout

Excessive or prolonged stress can, when left unchecked, gradually build up and eventually result in burnout; a state of emotional, mental, and physical exhaustion which, although not applying to experiences outside the workplace, can still affect all areas of a person's life.

Looking at the factors influencing contact with health services, the 11th Revision of the International

Classification of Diseases (ICD-11) describes burnout not as a medical condition, but as an occupational phenomenon. Burnout is defined as:

> a syndrome conceptualized as resulting from chronic workplace stress that has not been successfully managed. It is characterized by three dimensions:
>
> * feelings of energy depletion or exhaustion;
> * increased mental distance from one's job, or feelings of negativism or cynicism related to one's job;
> * reduced professional efficacy.
>
> Burn-out refers specifically to phenomena in the occupational context and should not be applied to describe experiences in other areas of life.

With burnout, problems seem insurmountable, everything looks bleak, and it's difficult to muster up the energy to care, let alone do something to help yourself. You probably feel that you're in over your head or have little control over the situation; you don't see any hope of positive change in your situation. Caring seems like a total waste of energy. You've run out of resources to cope. Pretty much every day is a bad day.

Emotional and physical responses:

* Lack of energy, exhaustion/extreme tiredness, mental fatigue
* Being unable to concentrate, increased emotional and cognitive distance from one's job
* Low mood, depressed, negative, anxious, irritable, tearful
* Frustrated, angry with work, workplace, and colleagues

- Disillusionment, resentment, bitterness, embitterment/cynicism related to one's job. Feeling unable to continue in the job
- Feeling traumatized, trapped, broken
- Dissociative feelings; emotionally cut off, empty, numb
- Hopelessness, helplessness, beyond caring, giving up, feeling at rock bottom.

How you might behave:

- Reduced performance at work
- Neglecting your own needs, either because you're too busy or you don't care anymore
- Little or no compassion for others, dismissive of others
- Inability to relate to others emotionally, distancing yourself from them
- Lack of energy or enthusiasm for interests outside of work.

Being super busy overloads us with stress and anxiety – Excessive 'busy-ness' is usually a sign that all is not well. When I'm reaching burnout I start fixing too many dates and writing too many e-mails. I become so uber-busy that things don't make sense anymore.

Ruby Wax

Trauma

According to the *Diagnostic and Statistical Manual of Mental Disorders*, trauma is defined as 'exposure to actual or threatened death, serious injury, or sexual violence; either directly, as a witness or by learning it happened to a loved one or friend'.

Trauma does not just happen to other people – it happens to us, our friends and family and our neighbours. While humans are an extremely resilient species, able to rebound from relentless wars, family violence and man-made disasters, experiences like these inevitably leave traces: on our minds, our emotions and even on our biology and immune systems. This matters not just to those who are directly affected, but to the people around them.

Bessel van der Kolk

There can be varying levels of trauma and traumatic stress. Whilst many individuals who are exposed to trauma can move on from it, for others it's not that simple. Trauma can leave ongoing symptoms that need professional support and psychotherapeutic intervention. Part of our brain can be good at denying the trauma has happened; however, the brain and the symptoms associated with the original trauma can be re-activated by a slight sense of danger.

Emotional and physical responses:

- Ruminating and replaying on a loop the memories in your mind
- Intrusive flashbacks and disturbing images and thoughts
- Feeling trapped in the past events

- Nightmares, waking in terror
- Anxiety and feeling on edge, fearful and constantly 'on guard', seeing danger everywhere
- Feeling out of control, vulnerable, hopeless, and helpless
- Feelings of despair and bleakness, sadness, depression, grief
- Survivors guilt, self-blame, and self-criticism
- Angry, violent outbursts
- Numbness and feeling empty.

How you might behave:

- Withdrawing from family/friends/loved ones/colleagues
- Avoiding things/people related to the traumatic event
- Difficulty trusting people
- Panic and being easily startled
- Inability to rest or relax
- Impulsive behaviour
- Panic attacks.

Life Changes and the Impact on Mental Health and Wellbeing

Our mental health and wellbeing can change not just from day to day, month to month, and year to year, but at key stages and changes in our lives. Childhood, adolescence, going into further or higher education, starting work, being in a relationship, becoming a parent, midlife, retirement etc. all have particular relevance and can impact on our wellbeing and mental health. Here we describe how some key life stages can adversely impact on mental health and we list common emotional and behavioural responses.

Menstruation and Mental Health

With menstruation comes hormonal changes that can cause emotional and physical symptoms each month. For some women these symptoms are mild and for others, distressing and difficult to manage.

Emotional responses:

* Mood swings, irritability, anxiety, frustration, anger
* Depression, sadness, crying
* Low confidence and self-esteem.

How you might behave:

* Inability to focus and concentrate or achieve as much as usual
* Withdrawing from groups and social activities
* Being irrational and impulsive
* Abandoning normal physical activity
* Greater inclination to conflict with others; easily offended.

'Periods can be a problem for female tennis players. I often lose if I'm on my period. I suffer when I have it. I always have one bad day when I'm tired, I have no energy and all I want is sugar. Playing at Wimbledon, with its all-white dress code, makes things even more difficult. You're in short skirts and tiny shorts. It's the worst thing – and so distracting.'

Heather Watson. Tennis player

Menopause and Mental Health

When a woman experiences menopause, her ovaries stop producing the hormones – oestrogen and progesterone – that contribute to the reproductive system's normal cycle. This can result in distressing and uncomfortable physical, psychological, and emotional symptoms. (Some individuals who have transitioned from female to male may still have their ovaries, and so may also experience menopausal symptoms.)

Some women see menopause as a positive experience, no longer having to be concerned about periods or pregnancy, and see middle age as a time to think of themselves rather than dependents. But for others, menopause can be felt as a loss; a woman may feel that a part of their life is over; that she doesn't compare so well with younger family members and colleagues.

Emotional responses:
- Mood swings – anger, sadness, irritability
- Anxiety, depression
- Low self-esteem/confidence
- Feelings of hopelessness

- Nervousness
- Panic/feeling trapped
- Loss of identity – 'I don't know who I am any more'
- Suicidal thoughts/feelings

How you might behave:

- Inability to concentrate at work
- Feeling confused and unable to prioritize
- Lack of interest in usual social activities
- Being argumentative and irritable, less patient with self and others
- Memory lapses in conversation with others
- Eating more – comfort eating

Male Midlife and Mental Health

People joke about the male 'mid-life crisis' and of men they know who have left their partners for someone much younger than themselves, or bought themselves a motorbike or a sports car. For some men, middle age makes them acutely aware that part of their life is over; they may feel they don't compare so well with younger family members and colleagues. They may either attempt to regain their youth or sink into a depression.

Although, as with any life stage, there are positive aspects to middle age, men too struggle, just as women do, with changes and challenges in life; mental health statistics and suicide rates for men certainly reflect this. (And some individuals who have transitioned from male to female may still experience difficulties specific to their gender identity, or original birth identity.)

You spend the first 20 years of your life running, running, running. You reach a point where you question if you can keep running like this for another 20 years.

Paolo Gallo

Emotional responses:

- Depression and anxiety
- Negativity, pessimism, and hopelessness
- Irritability
- Sadness for life that has passed
- A sense of needing to cram more into life – time is running out
- Suicidal thoughts/feelings.

How you might behave:

- Becoming withdrawn from friends and family
- May want to leave everything – partner, job, family, country, without thinking through the consequences
- Disengagement from work
- Spending more time at work as a displaced behaviour/anxiously avoiding relationships
- Becoming more selfish and self-centred
- Becoming more erratic and unable to think clearly
- Increased alcohol or recreational drug intake
- Eating more/less.

Grief and Mental Health

Grief is normal human response to loss. As well as being a response to the death or loss of loved ones – people or pets – grief can be a response to the loss of anyone or anything that we have had an emotional attachment to. Grief – profound feelings of loss – can be a response to a range of life changes – to divorce, family moving away, the loss of a job, or loss of a social group. It can also be a response to the diagnosis of a health problem, which results in a change in autonomy, identity, and/or physical appearance.

How we each manage and cope with grief is influenced by gender, cultural, philosophical, and spiritual beliefs. As well as being a cognitive and emotional response, grief is also experienced physically. Physical aches and pains such as chest pain or aching are common, as are feelings of being unable to breathe. Feelings can vary in intensity over time.

Emotional responses:

* Deep despair that is triggered easily by reminders
* Fearing harm to oneself and others, fearing a repeat of a similar loss
* Fear of being left alone
* Fear of breaking down, or losing control
* Anxiety
* Intense sadness, crying and sobbing
* Anger
* Mood swings

- Helplessness/powerlessness
- Shock, numbness, a sense of things being 'unreal' or 'surreal'
- Sense of longing
- Feeling let down and abandoned
- Guilt or shame
- Spiritual beliefs may be challenged
- Sense of 'what's the point', meaninglessness of life
- Feeling suicidal, sometimes wanting to join the person who has died
- Loss of perspective on other life issues.

How you might behave:

- Withdrawing from close family and friends
- Being aggressive to others/argumentative
- Impulsiveness
- Inability to talk about other subjects, constantly returning to issues of loss
- Inability to concentrate on daily tasks
- 'Ignoring grief' and 'pushing through it'
- Refusal to get up from bed
- Impatience with self and others
- Using or increase in use of alcohol, recreational drugs, cigarettes.

In terms of that horrific pain and inability to see that life will ever be the same again – yes grief does end. Do you get over grief? Absolutely you do – with love. Is there joy? Absolutely. But in those early days I never thought grief would end. In my case, it took quite a period of time. Those first 5 years. . .grief is very shocking. I miss her every single day.

Joely Richardson. Actor

Although Joely says, that for her, 'grief does end', many people experience the death of a loved one and subsequent feelings of grief differently. Their description is that they learn to live without their loved one and find a 'new kind of normal' in their lives. It has been described by some as a 'slow healing quarry of grief'.

The grief is not always present for them, but there are times that, as one person has said, 'I drop into my grief, with the same intensity, as if it happened yesterday'.

2

Is Work Good for Your Mental Health and Wellbeing?

The most important contributors to a life in good health, including mental health, are to have a job that provides a sufficient income, a decent and safe home and a support network. More simply put – a job, a home and a friend.
Duncan Selbie.
Chief Executive, Public Health England

In 2006, the UK's Department for Work and Pensions published an independent review *Is Work Good for Your Health and Wellbeing?* The reviewers – Gordon Waddell and A. Kim Burton – set out to answer the question 'Does the current evidence suggest that work is beneficial for physical and mental health and well being, in general and for common health problems?'

The conclusion was 'Yes, work is generally good for the physical and mental health and well-being of healthy people, many disabled people and most people with common health problems.' And in answer to the question, 'What is the balance of benefits and risks to health from work and from worklessness?' the reviewers stated that 'In general, provided due care is taken to make jobs as safe and "good" as reasonably practicable, employment can promote health and well-being, and the benefits outweigh any "risks" of work and the adverse effects of (long-term) unemployment or sickness absence'.

The Health and Safety Executive's Management Standards

Work might be good for you but what makes for good work? In describing what makes for a good job, one person will differ from another in the weight they place on factors such as salary, workload, level of responsibility, working environment, convenience of location, opportunities for career progression etc., but there *are* some minimum requirements for all of us.

In 2004, the Health and Safety Executive (HSE) – the agency responsible for the research, advice, regulation, and enforcement of workplace health, safety, and welfare – established a set of 'Management Standards'. These standards are concerned with what can be considered reasonable requirements of the following six aspects of a person's job:

Demands: Employees are able to cope with the demands of their jobs. Includes issues like workload, work patterns, and the work environment.

Control: Employees are able to have a say about the way they do their work.

Support: Employees receive adequate information and support. This includes the encouragement, sponsorship, and resources provided by the organization, line management, and colleagues.

Relationships: The focus here is on promoting positive working to avoid conflict and dealing with unacceptable behaviour; employees are not subjected to unacceptable behaviours, for example, bullying at work.

Role: Employees understand their role and responsibilities and the organization ensures that the person does not have conflicting roles.

Change: Employees feel that the organization engages them frequently when undergoing an organizational change.

The HSE suggests that if these six standards are effectively managed, employees will experience a good level of health and wellbeing. On the other hand, mismanagement of any of these six key areas of a person's job can lead to stress, poor health, low productivity, and increased accident and sickness rates at work.

In other words, unmanageable workloads or demands, unclear job roles and responsibilities, a lack of support, an unhealthy work–life balance, poor relationships with a manager, colleagues (and clients or customers) not being consulted or informed about changes at work – all these factors can have a negative impact on a person's wellbeing and mental health. And, suggest

HSE, they are exacerbated if there are no systems in place to respond to any individual concerns.

The mental health organization Mind add that other factors that can contribute towards stress and mental health problems in the workplace are:

* long hours and no breaks
* inability to use annual leave
* a poor physical working environment
* high-risk roles
* lone working
* job insecurity
* financial worries.

Review of the Health of Britain's Working Age Population

Even though the HSE's Management Standards identified what makes for healthy, productive working conditions, putting those standards into practice has been another matter. In 2008, Dame Carol Black's *Review of the Health of Britain's Working Age Population* was published. It identified some of the challenges that employers faced in creating healthy workplaces. 'The aim of the Review,' wrote Dame Carol who was National Director for Work and Health 'is not to offer a utopian solution for improved health in working life. Rather it is to identify the factors that stand in the way of good health and to elicit interventions, including changes in attitudes, behaviours and practices – as well as services – that can help overcome them.'

The review found that amongst the challenges was the fact that:

- 'Evidence to support the business case for investment in the health and well-being of their employees is inadequately understood by employers.
- There is a lack of appropriate information and advice to enable employers to invest in the health and well-being of their employees.'

Dame Carol proposed that a shift in attitude was necessary to ensure that employers and employees 'recognise not only the importance of preventing ill-health, but also the key role the workplace can play in promoting health and wellbeing'.

Two of the key recommendations were for:

- the need to recognize the role of the workplace in health and wellbeing;
- the need to develop professional expertise for working age health.

Dame Carol also recommended that there was a need for better understanding by employers of 'the economic case for investing in health and well-being' and also a need to explore 'practical ways to make it easier for smaller employers and organizations to establish health and well-being initiatives'.

Thriving at Work Review

In 2017, an independent review, *Thriving at Work* – led by mental health campaigner Lord Dennis Stevenson and Paul Farmer, Chief Executive at Mind and chair of the NHS Mental Health Taskforce – suggested that the Health and Safety Executive should do more to increase employers' awareness of their duties to manage wellbeing and mental health at work. Stevenson and Farmer found that employers often focus solely on physical safety and health. 'This should not be the case, and there is no such limitation in the Health and Safety at Work Act', they said. 'HSE's guidance could provide a more holistic approach.'

The *Thriving at Work* review set out a framework of core standards that all UK employers, it suggests – no matter what their size or the industry in which they operate – can implement to address workplace wellbeing and mental health.

These 'core standards' are for employers to:

- implement a mental health at work plan;
- develop mental health awareness among employees;
- encourage open conversations about mental health and available support;
- provide good working conditions and ensure employees have a healthy work–life balance;
- promote effective people management through line managers and supervisors;
- monitor employee mental health and wellbeing.

Four additional 'enhanced' standards have been outlined for large employers and the public sector who 'can and should do more to lead the way', according to the review.

These are to:

- increase transparency and accountability through internal and external reporting;
- demonstrate accountability;
- improve the disclosure process;
- ensure provision of tailored in-house mental health support and signposting to clinical help.

Employers should risk assess and manage work-related mental ill-health in the same way as they would work-related physical ill-health. We recommend that the HSE revise its guidance to raise employer awareness of their duty to assess and manage work-related mental ill-health.

Thriving at Work

Work and Stress

Issues such as a poor working environment, unrealistic deadlines, poor communication, poor interpersonal relationships, too much responsibility, and a lack of management support can significantly impact on the wellbeing of people at work. People get stressed. Especially if they're also dealing with difficulties and problems outside of work. People get stressed when they feel overwhelmed or unable to cope as a result of pressures and demands that are unmanageable; when they feel they have little control over a situation.

The 2018 TUC biennial survey of union health and safety representatives showed that the five most frequently cited hazards of main concern in the workplace were: stress; bullying/harassment; overwork; back strains; and slips, trips, and falls on the level. As with the 2016 survey, stress stood out as being the dominant health and safety concern.

Typically, when employees do go off sick as a result of stress, managers and employers are not aware that stress is the reason. Recent research by Mind reports that when asked how workplace stress had affected them, more than one in five (21%) said that they had called in sick to avoid work. Ninety per cent of people who have called in sick because of stress say they have given a different reason.

Speaking at an Investors In People Health & Wellbeing Seminar in 2015 Dame Carol Black said: 'Very often what the GP will write on a medical certificate – because they have to write something – isn't really the truth. When I did the independent review on sickness absence for the government, I talked to lots of people who were collecting their sicknotes and what they said is: "I hate my line manager. I'm never going back to that job". But no GP I've ever known writes anything other than a "medical" diagnosis; the closest they get is "stress" or "anxiety" – often not the truth at all.

Stress (can be) the result of poor relations at work. But it (the medical certificate) never says "poor relations at work" or "bullying at work". Never.'

Investing in Employee Wellbeing and a Mentally Healthy Workplace

Mind report that poor mental health is now the number one reason for staff absence.

Every employer depends on having healthy and productive employees; valued and supported staff are far more likely to deliver the best outcomes for a business. It's not good business sense for employers to ignore the wellbeing and mental health of their staff. Not only can low levels of wellbeing and mental ill-health result in poor performance and productivity but poor wellbeing and mental health is now the number one cause of long-term sick leave amongst employees.

Everyone is somewhere on the mental health spectrum, so this is a business productivity issue, which should be dealt with alongside other health and safety considerations. Creating a positive environment for mental health demonstrably costs less than failing to do so.

Nigel Carrington. Vice Chancellor, University of the Arts

2018/2019 figures from the UK Labour Force Survey showed that 602,000 people reported that they were experiencing work-related stress, depression, or anxiety. This resulted in an average of 21.2 sick days per person. Stress, depression, or anxiety accounted for 44% of all work-related ill-health cases and 54% of all working days lost due to ill-health.

Talking at an Investors in People: Health & Wellbeing seminar in 2015, Dame Carol Black said: 'It's crucially important, as far as the employee is concerned, that a workplace is a good workplace where you can do good work. And if you don't have that, most of us respond just like ordinary human beings; we take away our discretionary effort – we just take it away. We may not think about it very much but if you're disillusioned, not feeling OK at work, why should you go the extra mile? It's just a very normal human reaction. And that can be disastrous. . .and so we absolutely need engaged staff at work.'

Workplaces that genuinely promote and value wellbeing and good mental health and support people with mental health problems are more likely to reduce absenteeism, improve engagement and retention of employees, increase productivity, and benefit from associated economic gains.

This strong relationship between levels of staff wellbeing, motivation, and business performance is often called 'employee engagement'. Employee engagement occurs when workplace conditions allow for everyone to give of their best, be committed to their organization's goals and values, motivated to contribute to organizational success; to feel valued and supported and have a positive sense of their own wellbeing.

By supporting staff wellbeing, employers reap the benefits through enhanced morale, loyalty, commitment, innovation, productivity, and profitability.

In the next four chapters, you will read how both employers and employees can promote and value wellbeing and mental health in ways that are beneficial to everyone.

3
How to Be a Good Place to Work

We need to move to a society where all of us become more aware of our own mental health, other people's mental health and how to cope with our own and other people's mental health when it fluctuates. It is all our responsibilities to make this change. However. . .employers are perhaps able to have the greatest impact and scope to make an impact.
Paul Farmer and Lord Dennis Stevenson.
Thriving at Work review

Employers bear the primary responsibility for establishing the conditions and practices in the workplace which minimise the likelihood of people being made ill by their jobs. . .there is also a compelling case for organisations of all sectors and sizes. . .to embed health and well-being at their heart and to create an empowering and rewarding work environment for all employees.
Dame Carol Black.
*Review of the Health of Britain's
Working Age Population*

Take Stock

As an employer, senior leader, or manager, in order to 'embed health and wellbeing at the heart' of your organization, you need to start by getting a clear picture of what factors may affect staff wellbeing and mental health in your workplace.

Of course, low morale is not difficult to spot. If you have unhappy employees, it will show. Pessimistic, resigned, and negative attitudes; conflict and a lack of cooperation between colleagues and/or management; little in the way of initiative, commitment, or enthusiasm from workers; a culture of criticism, complaints, blame, and resentment; covert conversations, gossip, and misinformation; high levels of absenteeism are all clear signs that things aren't right.

Under the Health and Safety at Work Act 1974 and the Management of Health and Safety at Work Regulations 1999, employers have a legal duty to protect employees from stress at work by doing a risk assessment and acting on it. The first step, then, is to gather information on the current state of staff wellbeing in the organization. This will provide evidence of the need for action and will give a baseline starting point from which to measure improvement once action is taken. You need to find out:

- what may be causing stress in your workplace;
- what approaches and strategies are already in place to support wellbeing and mental health in your workplace;
- how effective those approaches/strategies are.

Once you have that information, you're in a position to plan next steps. If, though, you don't take stock of your employees' mental wellbeing you won't have a true picture of what's really going on, which will mean that any steps you do take to reduce stress and improve wellbeing and mental health may be less effective.

The best way to find out what is and isn't working for people is, of course, to ask. Mind's publication *How to Take Stock of Mental Health in Your Workplace* provides practical advice on how to collect information about employees' wellbeing so that you can identify priorities for action. The Health and Safety Executive have a survey template you can use to gather information from your staff about their wellbeing. You can find this on their website. Go to hse.gov.uk and put 'Indicator Tool' into the search bar, then click on 'Work Related Stress Tools and Templates'.

The survey template has questions (based on the HSE Management Standards) about mental wellbeing at work, that aim to identify:

- how employees view the demands of the job;
- issues around the amount of control over their job that employees feel they have;
- issues around relationships at work;
- satisfaction with communication in the workplace;
- how employees view their job role and how supported they feel.

You can adapt the template and add any questions which may be specific to your workplace and staff.

Data from the questionnaire can be fed into an analysis tool which is also available on the HSE website. The analysis tool can be used to highlight any hotspots and prioritize areas for action. The questionnaire can be repeated at a later date to see what progress towards achieving the Standards has occurred.

The findings from the questionnaire should lead to proposals for practical change that must be implemented.

Remember, it is your duty to ensure that your employees are not made ill by their work. Failure to assess the risk of stress and mental health problems and to take steps to alleviate them could leave you open to costly compensation claims. Of course, the survey could uncover some uncomfortable truths, such as, in some cases, the need to address a long hours culture, or to increase staffing levels. That is why it is crucial to get commitment from the top.

Take Staff Wellbeing Seriously – From the Top

In the US, 73% of employees with senior managers who showed support through involvement and commitment to wellbeing initiatives said their organization helps employees develop a healthy lifestyle, compared with just 11% who work in an organization without that leadership support, according to the American Psychological Association's 2016 Work and Well-Being Survey.

Employees need to know that senior leaders and managers at all levels believe that the wellbeing of staff really does matter; that they are committed to providing the resources and doing whatever is necessary to implement the findings of a staff wellbeing survey.

Case Study

In 2016 Daniella Lang started as headteacher at Brimsdown Primary School in Enfield, North London, shortly after the school had received two 'requires improvement' inspections by Ofsted (Office for Standards in Education, Children's Services and Skills). The subsequent changes she and her leadership team made – a new English and phonics scheme, for example – and redundancies during the first year left staff morale low. Daniella decided to start a staff wellbeing team, and asked for volunteers from the teaching staff to help.

'The results', she wrote in the Guardian in February 2018, 'have been extraordinary. Two years later, our most recent Ofsted grade improved to "good" with three outstanding elements – and we're now in the top 20% for progress in reading and maths. Staff report they are much happier and the school has more of a family feel to it.

The first after-school meeting of the wellbeing team included some hard truths. Each attendee had the opportunity to be honest about how they felt. It was clear that the changes I had implemented had caused staff a great deal of stress, but they were still keen to engage with further training and development. While I was part of the problem, I also wanted to be part of the solution.'

The team distributed a wellbeing survey. The results showed that only 42% of staff felt they got the support they needed for their job and only 45% felt supported by their line manager. Twenty percent of staff didn't feel inspired to do their job.

'As well as dealing with change, there had been issues around fairness and consistency in the school, in terms of staff hours and overtime and behaviour expectations. We introduced procedures, including a behaviour policy, which went some way towards addressing this.

Other problems associated with workload, particularly on an administrative level, were helped by acquiring a second photocopier, employing an intern to help with laminating, and setting time aside during inset days to prepare resources.'

By ensuring all of the school's leadership team have an open-door policy – staff were encouraged to approach the team with any issues – prioritising staff training, and supporting the wellbeing team, 'I'm pleased to say,' wrote Daniella, 'our school is a much happier place for our staff to be.'

'Six months after we first issued the survey, we ran it again. Almost all (96%) of the school's staff felt inspired to do their job (this was despite support staff redundancies happening at the time), 96% felt supported by line managers and 100% of staff said they had friendships within work – all huge improvements from the March survey. They also felt much less stress. In January 2018, this stress level has gone down even further from a previous average score of 3.31 out of five to an average 2.43 out of five.

Now, staff are proud of where they work, feel supported and want to see the school go from strength to strength. Some members of the wellbeing team have left, others have stayed, but it remains a force for good in our school. I don't know how we'd get by without one.'

Daniella Lang's account clearly demonstrates a genuine commitment from a senior leader towards staff health and wellbeing. Perhaps as an employer or manager, you share that commitment but don't know where to start or what to do. You're not alone! Recent research by Mind discovered that 56% of employers said they would like to do more to improve staff wellbeing but don't feel they have the right training or guidance.

A major part of a manager's role is to support staff to do their job; to do their job well. In their 2016 report, *Growing the health and well-being agenda; from first steps to full potential*, the Chartered Institute of Personnel and Development (CIPD) state that 'Managers are pivotal in shaping employees' experience of work; they have a vital role to play in managing and enhancing employee well-being, but may lack confidence, experience or skills to promote mental health and well-being.' The report goes on to say: 'Training is vital to ensure that managers have a clear understanding of health and well-being policies and responsibilities, and have the confidence and interpersonal skills required to implement policies sensitively and fairly and have difficult conversations with individuals where appropriate.'

If I only had a small amount of money to spend. . . I would train my managers in people training.

Dame Carol Black

In 2019, speaking at a Health and Wellbeing at Work conference in Birmingham, Dame Carol emphasized that organizations should focus more on equipping managers with the skills needed to handle their teams' mental health concerns. And this support should not be limited to line managers – senior leaders and stakeholders should also be engaged in workplace wellbeing if they are to ensure a mentally healthy workplace. Black said: 'Please do put the fresh fruit and the bicycle schemes in, but please do not do it unless you've done leadership and stakeholder engagement and line manager capability [training], otherwise it's a sticking plaster.'

Two organizations that provide such training are Mind and the Advisory, Conciliation and Arbitration

Service (ACAS). Mind's Positive Mental Health in the Workplace eLearning is designed to support managers. For large organizations Mind license their eLearning courses to use as part of your learning management system. Mind also have a free eLearning course for people working in small workplaces. ACAS currently offer a one-day training course; 'Mental health in the workplace: skills for managers' which provides managers with the knowledge and practical skills to confidently and effectively manage mental health within their teams.

Another organization that provides training and support for managers is Time to Change. time-to-change.org.uk. Time to Change is a mental health campaign, launched in 2007. Their 'Employer Pledge and Employer Action Plan' supports employers to put in place best-practice interventions and policy to help your staff work in ways that promote positive mental wellbeing.

Time to Change offer training to line managers so that they feel comfortable having conversations about mental health with their line reports. Signing the Time to Change employer pledge is free and they offer dedicated support throughout the process as well as a year of support after you sign. This includes coaching on your action plan, connections to other employers, and free training where you can learn from leading employers how they have achieved success. Time to Change will also support you in recruiting employees to be mental health champions who will separately have access to training and peer support, as well as access to working groups that involve champions from other organizations.

Case Study

'Split the Bills' is a small organization employing 30 staff that provides a utility and household bill management service for rented student properties. In 2017, the company decided to make wellbeing and mental health a priority after a staff survey highlighted that 71% of their employees had experienced stress, low mood, or mental health problems while at work. Many did not know where to get support. Determined to create an environment where people could open up about their mental health, Split the Bills signed up for the Time to Change pledge.

As well as a number of workplace wellbeing initiatives – employees are encouraged to write up personal 'wellness action plans', there's a comfortable quiet room for when employees need a break from their desks, monthly walk and talks in the Peak District, 'curry and chat' nights, and regular mental health awareness events – with the support of Time to Change, the company recruited employee mental health champions; trained mental health first aiders – each of whom can signpost people to organizations offering professional help if needed.

Once again, commitment from senior leaders is vital in any organization that wishes to improve the wellbeing and mental health of their staff. If you need to make a business case to your senior leaders and budget holders Time to Change has put together a document *Business Case for Training* to help you get sign-off to deliver well-being and mental health training to staff.

Promote a Culture of Openness Around Wellbeing and Mental Health

People don't care how much you know until they know how much you care.

Teddy Roosevelt

Recent research carried out by Mind UK, found that 30% of staff did not agree with the statement 'I would feel able to talk openly with my line manager if I was feeling stressed'. Too often, employees are reluctant to talk to their manager and problems can spiral. Raising awareness and encouraging discussion of mental health and wellbeing helps to promote positive attitudes and expectations. And, most importantly, talking openly lets people know that they will get support if they're experiencing a mental health problem.

Talking about mental health and wellbeing can start at induction. When a new staff member is starting their job, provide information about what support is available for staff to look after their wellbeing and mental health.

Ongoing awareness raising could include:

- Putting up posters about wellbeing and mental health in your workplace; Mental Health at Work mentalhealthatwork.org.uk/ and Mind both have posters and top tips postcards that can be printed off.
- Information, ideas, and advice about wellbeing and mental health in staff newsletters, staff magazines, and intranet pages.
- Inviting a speaker on mental health to an event as part of activities for diversity, disability, or mental health awareness. Mind can help you with this; email them at work@mind.org.uk.

As a supervisor, manager, or team leader, speak regularly with staff to see how they're doing – how they're coping with their workload, relationships at work – and to identify what may be becoming stressful. Ensure appraisal and supervision procedures ask about mental wellbeing and stress. You could also establish a regular item in team meetings where people also talk about wellbeing, stress, and difficulties they may be experiencing. If your business has carried out a staff wellbeing survey, issues uncovered in the survey could form the basis of the discussion. Whether it has or hasn't carried out a survey, a regular item in meetings could be for you to simply ask:

- What, if anything, has been stressful recently at work? What might make things easier?
- What, if anything, has contributed to positive wellbeing?

I never thought other colleagues were suffering in silence too – the mental health awareness training brought about a more open discussion in the following weeks and months – I had no idea other people in my team were also impacted by ill health before this. Just to know my workplace take this seriously and are compassionate means I now feel I can speak about what I know are early warning signs (only to a few people – but that's enough) that I am becoming anxious – it's stopped the vicious cycle gaining speed and taking over.

Senior Nurse. Brighton and Sussex University Hospitals NHS Trust

For those staff working in isolation – lone workers – monthly team meetings or regular phone catch-ups are important. And, for some people, talking in front of others can be difficult or isn't always appropriate, so do create additional opportunities for communication. Regular one-to-one meetings – an informal chat or a more formal meeting – can help to identify issues early so employees can get the relevant support. Chats and meetings also provide the opportunity for people to talk about personal issues that may be affecting them such as health concerns, family issues, financial worries, or other personal matters which might be contributing to them struggling at work.

Encouraging and normalizing open conversations about mental health and wellbeing can help staff to think more about and better manage their own wellbeing and mental health and their ability to empathize and support others.

Inform Staff, Listen to Staff, and Involve Them with Decision-making

As well as encouraging a culture of openness around wellbeing and mental health, as far as possible, there needs to be a culture of openness about what's happening at work; new directions, initiatives, changes etc. Keeping staff informed about what's happening – with their team, in their department and other departments, what the company's short and long-term goals are, how the company is doing – is a simple way to build trust, create and maintain a shared goal or purpose. Confusion, worry, and stress occur when employees feel uninformed about what's going on. They're likely to fill in the gaps with gossip and untruths.

From the start, employees need to know and understand what is expected of them; what rules, procedures, practices, or policies they're expected to comply with. All these things need to be written down and be easily accessible. A company intranet is a good place to store information; the policies, documents, and forms that employees frequently need or ask for. It's also a good place to archive newsletters and updates.

Ongoing communication should include different types of media; simply relying on email may result in some staff not being included, e.g. cleaners/housekeepers, ancillary workers, and those without regular access to computers at work.

Good communication with employees centres around delivering relevant, timely, and consistent information to all. It relies upon everybody being in the loop. However, in an attempt to keep them continually informed. you need to be careful not to overload staff with too much information about anything and everything. Too many meetings, emails, notifications, and alerts that are irrelevant result in people either getting stressed by too much information – there's just too much to take in and process – and/or switching off. Then they miss the important information that is relevant to them.

The way to avoid information overload and to get the balance right is simply to get feedback from staff. Ask people, individually, in team meetings and in staff surveys and questionnaires, how they feel about levels of communication from senior leaders, managers, and colleagues.

Aim to involve all staff in decision-making; not only about what and how they do their job but, where possible, about the direction of the organization and how to address challenges and problems so they can contribute to solutions.

Encourage ideas and suggestions. This might be a physical box or it might be a designated email address or online form. Make sure that ideas and suggestions are responded to. Explain if, how, and when people's suggestions will be acted on and if the idea isn't right at the time explain why you aren't using it. If employees see that their suggestions and ideas are rarely responded to or acted on, they'll stop submitting them.

> **Case Study**
>
> Livewell Southwest – a Plymouth-based organization delivering health and social care services that employs over 3000 staff – has a staff engagement council called Our Voice which enables staff to influence the future direction of the organization and debate current issues that affect the business it is engaged in.
>
> Livewell Southwest says: 'By sharing their views and debating issues affecting our work, feedback gathered via Our Voice can influence our strategy, services and how we reinvest in the local communities we serve. Our Voice is integral to maintaining the high-quality service we provide to local communities and Livewell Southwest hugely values the contributions made by our teams. Our staff represent the communities that they live in and it is important that they can influence the organisation. An Our Voice representative attends our board meetings, providing employee insight and reflection.'

Good communication with staff is especially important when there are changes in the workplace. For some types of change, formal consultation may be necessary, with opinions and suggestions sought and considered (ACAS and the Trades Union Congress (TUC) have information on this). But even when a formal consultation isn't involved, people do need to know about the change.

The management of change is one of the Health and Safety Executive's six standards; it recommends that: 'the organisation ensures adequate employee consultation on changes and provides opportunities for employees to influence proposals'.

Managing any change effectively depends on ensuring employees understand what's happening and how it may affect them, and receive answers to concerns. Employees need to know:

- Why changes are necessary – what happened to prompt the change – what the goal is.
- What changes will be made, by whom, how, and when.
- How it will impact on employees and their work; how people will benefit.
- The challenges; what support and resources will be available to help smooth the transitions.

When a change becomes evident and employees have not been informed, they're likely to fill the void with negative information, which can create all sorts of further problems. Often, people would rather hear bad news than no news. Regular communication and information can save a lot of time and effort correcting assumptions, half-truths, and inaccurate information that spring up if issues around changes at work aren't communicated appropriately. If people are informed and encouraged to be part of the change there is less resistance. So you'll need to invite and respond to questions and comment, ideas and suggestions. When employees are involved in finding solutions they feel trusted and respected and that their views are valued. They see that they have influence and that their opinions and ideas matter. they have some ownership of the final decision.

Despite the organisation going through large-scale organisational change with the prospect of people losing their jobs being very real, a couple of conditions meant this didn't have a negative impact. Firstly, we had a day's training on personal resilience and we were advised about online resources we could access. Secondly, our line manager made sure the team still had fun at work. He encouraged us to chat when we felt down, made sure the team laughed together, spent time together away from the office and actively asked how we were. Our manager encourages us to bring all components of what makes us who we are to the workplace. I have felt accepted, understood and happy.

Liz. An employee with a public sector organization

Encourage a Healthy Work–Life Balance

A recent Mental Health Foundation survey found that:

- One third of respondents feel unhappy or very unhappy about the time they devote to work.

- More than 40% of employees are neglecting other aspects of their life because of work, which may increase their vulnerability to mental health problems.
- When working long hours more than a quarter of employees feel depressed (27%), one third feel anxious (34%), and more than half feel irritable (58%).
- The more hours you spend at work, the more hours outside of work you are likely to spend thinking or worrying about it.
- As a person's weekly hours increase, so do their feelings of unhappiness.

The survey also found that nearly two-thirds of employees have experienced a negative effect on their personal life, including lack of personal development, physical and mental health problems, and poor relationships and poor home life.

For most people, working long hours for short periods is manageable. But over time, constant pressure and a poor work–life balance can quickly lead to stress and burnout.

Case Study

In 2018 IG Metall, Germany's biggest trade union representing metal and engineering workers, won a key victory in their push for a better work–life balance. The union struck a deal with the employers' federation, Südwestmetall, to give 900,000 industrial employees in Baden-Württemberg – home to Daimler, the carmaker, and Bosch – the right to work a reduced week.

Workers will be allowed to reduce their working week from the standard 35 hours to 28, for up to two years, in order to care for family members while preserving the right to return to full-time work. In return, companies will be able to offer more 40-hour-a-week contracts, at times when there is a shortage of skilled workers.

'Employees have more opportunities to reduce their hours of work, while companies get more options to increase the volume of working hours', said Stefan Wolf, Südwestmetall's negotiator.

'More and more people have periods in their lives when they want to work less, for example to look after elderly relatives, or to take a sabbatical or unpaid leave', Hanna Schwander, professor of public policy at the Hertie School of Governance in Berlin, told the UK's Financial Times. 'It is becoming,' she said, 'increasingly important for people to reconcile their personal and professional lives.'

'The agreement is a milestone on the way to a modern, self-determined world of work', IG Metall leader Jörg Hofmann told the BBC. IG Metall's agreements tend to be seen as benchmarks for the whole of German industry, and it is now expected to be rolled out in other sectors.

In the same year that IG Metall succeeded in its push for rights to reduced working hours, in New Zealand, in an eight-week trial, Perpetual Guardian, a financial services company, switched its 240 staff from a five-day to a four-day week and maintained their pay. Productivity increased by 20% in the four days they worked so there was no drop in the total amount of work done, a study of the trial revealed. Scores given by workers showed that staff stress levels were down from 45% to 38%. Work–life balance scores increased from 54% to 78%.

'This is an idea whose time has come', said Andrew Barnes, Perpetual Guardian's founder and chief executive. 'We need to get more companies to give it a go. They will be surprised at the improvement in their company, their staff and in their wider community.'

The trial was monitored by academics at the University of Auckland and Auckland University of Technology and according to Jarrod Haar, a professor of human resource management at the University of Technology, 'Beyond wellbeing, employees reported their teams were stronger and functioned better together, more satisfied with their jobs, more engaged and they felt their work had greater meaning', he said. 'They also reported being more committed to the organisation and less likely to look elsewhere for a job.'

Of course, where being present is a key part of the job for people working in frontline occupations such as nursing or the police, cutting their hours without reducing the public service they provide is not a practical option. However, there are other ways of creating and maintaining a healthy work–life balance.

Flexible working is one such way. Flexible working describes any type of working arrangement that gives some degree of flexibility on how long, where, and when employees work. With flexible work schedules, employees are able to fit their lives around their work, helping them balance personal lives – responsibilities and commitments – with their work lives.

ACAS points out that, 'As employers, organisations have a "duty of care" to protect their employees from risks to their health and safety. These risks might include stress caused by working long hours or struggling to balance work and home life. Flexible working can help to improve the health and well-being of employees and, by extension, reduce absenteeism, increase productivity, and enhance employee engagement and loyalty. . .With developments in technology, particularly in the availability of communication tools (such as fast home broadband and smart phones), more and more roles could be compatible with some forms of flexible working arrangement.'

ACAS's 'Flexible Working and Work Life Balance' guide (available at acas.org.uk) outlines important considerations for employers of all sizes who are considering flexible working practices.

Whatever the hours and whenever the hours that people work, they need to take proper lunch breaks.

'At Amstrad the staff start early and finish late. Nobody takes lunches – they may get a sandwich slung on their desk', Alan Sugar told an audience at City University in 1987. 'There's no small-talk. It's all action.' Are Lord Sugar's remarks outdated? In some workplaces, taking a proper lunch break and leaving work on time may still be seen as not being as committed as others who stay behind to work longer. But if your staff aren't taking proper breaks, chances are your company culture is not break-friendly.

If, for example, staff know that managers work late or they see managers working through lunch, they may feel that this is expected of them too. But if managers take lunch breaks and leave on time, they'll be more likely to follow suit.

We have a soup maker in the kitchen and once a week, a different staff member makes soup for everyone. In the summer, we make smoothies.

Pari. Retail worker

If possible, provide a quiet break area. While you can't impose a healthy eating regime, provide healthy snacks to encourage a culture of healthy eating to accompany a healthier attitude to taking breaks.

For breaks to be effective, there needs to be a change of pace that allows your staff to leave their work. So if you can persuade staff who work indoors to get outside for a bit of fresh air, even better. Another good idea is subsidizing fitness classes away from the workplace. Giving people gym memberships and encouraging them to make use of the gym during two or three lunchtimes every week is 'a good idea, not just because that person will keep fit, but because they'll be out of the office', says Cary Cooper, Professor of Organizational Psychology at Manchester Business School.

Encourage additional breaks. There are stressful periods in everyone's jobs, so make it clear to employees that if they need to take an extra break for some fresh air, they can and that their lunch break will be not be affected.

In fact, employees should be encouraged to regularly take a break and move around a bit. If people's jobs involve them spending long periods of every day sitting down, they're classed as 'sedentary' and at risk of health problems. The UK's 2016 government publication *Health Matters: Getting every adult active everyday* recommends that we should break up long periods of sitting time with short bouts of activity every 30 minutes. 'As well as being physically active, all adults are advised to minimise the time spent being sedentary (sitting) for extended periods. . .Spending large amounts of time sedentary increases the risk of adverse health outcomes.' It goes on to suggest that we should reduce the amount of time we sit during our working day by taking regular time not sitting during work and finding ways to break up sedentary time.

But if sitting is the problem, could standing be the solution? Apparently not. Whether you sit or stand, it's being in one position that's the problem. So as far as is practical, encourage sedentary employees to take frequent breaks that involve moving (more on this in Chapter 4).

Case Study

Livewell Southwest provide integrated health and social care services for people in the Southwest of England. Angela Saxby, Head of HR & Staff Wellbeing says: 'Our annual staff survey indicated that for some employees taking a break during the work day seemed out of the question. To start addressing the issue we ran a campaign to encourage employees to take a break. The campaign was kicked off by our Executive Team who wanted to role model from the top.

We had many teams sharing their ideas and posting pictures on how they promote wellbeing during the working day. Some examples included team lunches, going for a brisk walk, reading a book, listening to music and mindfulness.'

It could be that employees regularly work throughout their lunch, come in early, or work late because they've got too much to do. Managers need to monitor their employees' workloads to ensure that each person can do their work within their contracted hours. Employees must feel able to speak up if the demands placed on them are too great. They must also be encouraged to switch off when they leave work; to relax and recharge before returning to work the next day. Amongst other things, this means not taking work calls or checking their emails outside of office hours. Or does it?

Banning staff from accessing their work emails outside office hours could do more harm than good to employee wellbeing, according to a 2019 study published in the journal *Computers in Human Behaviour*. Dr Emma Russell, a senior lecturer in management at the University of Sussex Business School, says that, despite the best intentions of policies limiting email use, preventing people from working at times that best suit them could cause stress. She says: 'Employees need to feel free to respond to a "growing accumulation of emails", or they could end up feeling even more stressed and overloaded.'

Commenting on the research findings, Louise Aston, Wellbeing Campaign Director at Business in the Community, agreed: 'Working parents may prefer to respond to an email after the children are in bed and having restrictions on email could actually add to their stress levels', Aston said. 'There are often many barriers to employees taking up workplace initiatives, and we need to listen to staff to understand what their wellbeing needs are.'

CIPD Head of Public Policy Ben Willmott told BBC News: 'Employers need to provide clear guidance on remote working, including on the use of email and other forms of digital communication, to ensure that if people are accessing emails out of hours they are doing so because it suits them.'

People who regularly go home strung out and tired and do little, if anything, to de-stress, unwind, and relax come back to work the next day feeling no better; they still feel stressed and exhausted. Encouraging staff to rest and recuperate – particularly after busy periods – can start by simply asking them what they plan to do to unwind and recharge; what positive, healthy things they plan to do. Then encourage them to do just that.

As well as encouraging people to take breaks at work, rest and relax at the end of the day and on their days off, people need to take their annual leave. Many businesses have busy periods in the year when they need all hands on deck and they'd rather employees did not take holiday at these times. And in small businesses, too many employees taking holiday at the same time will leave them short staffed and have a detrimental effect on the business. But aside from these circumstances, employees should be encouraged to take annual leave. So, do have a clear policy and make it a straightforward process to book time off work.

Provide Opportunities for Learning and Development

A large part of the success of a business depends on all staff – whatever their role – having the relevant skills, knowledge, and abilities. But as well as having a workforce with up-to-date skills and knowledge, organizations that promote staff learning and skills development show that they believe that their staff and the work they do are worth investing in.

Annual appraisals are an obvious time to talk about learning and development interests, needs, and opportunities. But annual appraisals don't have to be the only time; learning and development should be an ongoing consideration.

As an employer or manager you may have certain things you want people to learn, but they might have other ideas. Find out what skills they want to learn and the knowledge and experience they want to develop and do ask how they see it benefiting them, their work, and the organization. A personal development plan can be useful. It sets out what the employee's agreed learning and development needs are, how and when they'll be achieved. Simply Google 'Personal Development Plan Template' to find a template you can download and use.

Be aware, though, that not everyone will always want to develop and progress; some people may just want to work in their current job and stay in that position. As long as an employee is doing their job well enough, they shouldn't be pressured into taking up learning and development opportunities.

Whatever your line of business or profession, with a bit of research, you can probably find a range of training opportunities – workshops and courses – from external trainers or online. Opportunities for learning and development can also be done in-house by using current skills and knowledge of individual staff members to train, coach, and mentor other staff and to provide job-shadowing opportunities. It's likely that there's a wealth of skills, knowledge, and experience available within your business. Mentoring schemes allow you to tap into that knowledge and make it available to others in your organization. Peer support encourages constructive working relationships with your staff, enabling colleagues to support one another outside of the line-management structure.

Mentoring and buddy schemes can help a new employee understand workplace systems, procedure, and policies and culture better, helping them to settle fit in more easily and quickly. The Chartered Management Institute have a downloadable guide, *Developing a Mentoring Scheme*, available at www.managers.org.uk and the short book *Effective Mentoring: Understand the skills and techniques of a successful mentor*, by Gill Hasson is also useful.

Another learning and development strategy is workshadowing. When employees shadow different employees and different teams, this provides access and insights that can help inform and support each other's jobs. Workshadowing helps to:

- break down barriers and myths about how others work;

- provide the opportunity to observe good practice elsewhere;
- provide fresh ideas and insights;
- allow good practice to be brought back to the shadow's current role;
- encourage the realization that other people have different ways of doing things;
- improve communication within the organization;
- provide networking opportunities and bring people together who might not normally have contact;
- increase understanding of the wider institutional goals and objectives.

There are no hard and fast rules for the time period involved; however, in most cases, a one-day or two-half-day time period could be practical.

Establish and Promote Positive Working Relationships and Social Activities

The 2017 *Thriving at Work* review recommends that employers 'take positive action to make the workplace a mutually supportive environment where good work relationships thrive'. When done right, mentoring and buddying and work shadowing schemes can help do just that. There are, of course, other ways to promote positive working relationships.

Do you, for example, take time to greet staff in the morning and say goodbye when they leave? Do you ask them how they are feeling if they have been off sick recently? These sorts of things are easy to do and go a long way.

So does letting someone know as soon as they do good work (rather than waiting until the next one-to-one meeting) It can develop a culture of praise which helps staff feel their efforts are recognized and keeps lines of communication open.

In 2018, employee benefit company Perkbox carried out a survey of two thousand adults in part-time and full-time employment. They compiled a list of 50 of the most commonly offered employee benefits and asked people to rate them out of one hundred. The top five most popular perks all involved social activities with colleagues. They were:

- extracurricular clubs (e.g. arts and crafts, book clubs)
- pool table
- ping-pong table
- office sports teams (e.g. football or netball)
- video games.

Positive working relationships can be supported by social activities that bring people together. Here are some ideas:

- Use health related activities for team building that boosts both physical health and mental wellbeing, for example, charity fundraisers involving physical activities, shared 'healthy' lunches, a lunchtime walking or running club, a lunchtime quiz related to health issues (for example BUPA bupa.co.uk have a healthy eating quiz. They also have a physical activity quiz to test knowledge about how much physical activity we should all be doing.)

- Have some 'Lunch and Learn' lunchtimes. Your organization provides the food for lunch and a speaker or instructor for, for example, yoga or Pilates sessions, or creative activities: calligraphy, sketching, magic tricks, bird watching, juggling.
- Designate an area for lunchtime board games such as chess, Scrabble, draughts, Mahjong, Risk, backgammon, and Battleship. Introduce a competitive element by dividing participants into teams such as Accounting vs. Customer Service.
- Set up some workplace challenges; for example, use step counters to see who – or which team – has walked the furthest in a week.
- Organize a weekend or evening walk which includes bringing your dog, children, parents, or partner.
- Organize evening get-togethers that involve activities such as dancing or bowling, rather than just drinking.
- Get together for a good cause; organize volunteer days. Volunteering gives workers an opportunity to create and strengthen bonds while making a contribution to their community. Go to do-it.org/news/using-your-work-volunteer-days for information and ideas.

Whatever the activities, aim to be inclusive. Employees should not be or feel excluded because of their level of physical ability, cultural or religious beliefs, race, sexuality, ability, age, or gender.

What makes for good morale and positive working relationships? When your workplace puts people first. Staff are comfortable; if there's a difficult situation, they're not worried about making a mistake, because they know they're supported; they're not automatically going to be reprimanded or the problem dismissed.

Tom. Booking agent

People need to feel psychologically safe. Organizational behavioural scientist Amy Edmondson of Harvard University first introduced the concept of 'team psychological safety' in the 1990s and defined it as 'a shared belief held by members of a team that the team is safe for interpersonal risk taking'.

In a team with high psychological safety, each person feels safe to take risks and be vulnerable around others. They feel comfortable expressing themselves and feel safe that no-one will undermine them, embarrass or punish anyone else for bringing up problems and tough issues, for speaking out about concerns, making and/or admitting a mistake, asking a question, asking for help, or offering a new idea.

If team members frequently do not feel they are in a group that is safe for interpersonal risk-taking, motivation, morale, creativity, and even innovation can drop.

Dr Jacinta Jiménez. Psychologist

Being able to feel safe with other people is probably the single most important aspect of mental health; safe connections are fundamental to meaningful and satisfying lives.

Bessel van der Kolk, MD. Psychiatrist

There needs to be a zero tolerance approach to bullying and harassment. ACAS report that 'research has consistently shown that workplace bullying is most common in environments with poor workplace climates. It is most often instigated by someone in a more powerful position than the target, frequently directed downward from a manager or senior manager to a subordinate.'

Case Study

My manager, who I worked very closely with on every aspect of my job, micromanaged everything that I did. Worse still, rather than being a boss who mentored, encouraged, and opened doors for me, despite her knowing I was a diligent and hard-working individual (other members of staff said so) – she did not want me to succeed, but she also did not want me to leave her as I worked so hard. Maybe she was afraid I would upstage her or too many people were noticing how well I did my job.

I would feel miles outside her inner circle, and not know why – despite us needing to function as a two-person team. She would keep good assignments to herself, especially if they involved contact with senior-level stakeholders. She had zero conversations with me about my forward path. I just didn't know what I'd done wrong.

I stayed for almost 2 years but this came at a massive cost to my mental health, especially my confidence. In hindsight, with more experience in both personal and professional life, I can now see that my manager saw me as a threat, but at the time I felt incredibly sad, not good enough and quite neurotic with questioning why doesn't she like me/what have I done wrong. Imagine how good I would have been if our relationship had been a positive one!

Liz. Employee at a design practice

Everyone should be treated with dignity and respect at work. Bullying and harassment of any kind are in no-one's interest and absolutely should not be tolerated in the workplace.

Bullying is often used as an umbrella term for both sets of behaviour. There is a distinction. The Equality Act 2010 defines harassment as 'unwanted conduct related to a relevant protected characteristic, which has the purpose or effect of violating an individual's dignity or creating an intimidating, hostile, degrading, humiliating or offensive environment for that individual'. The relevant protected characteristics are age, disability, gender re-assignment, race, religion or belief, sex, and sexual orientation.

ACAS characterizes bullying as 'offensive, intimidating, malicious or insulting behaviour, an abuse or misuse of power through means that undermine, humiliate, denigrate or injure the recipient'. The impact on the individual can be the same as harassment. However, unless bullying amounts to conduct defined as harassment in the Equality Act 2010 it is not possible to make a complaint to an Employment Tribunal about it.

There needs to be a zero tolerance approach to both bullying and harassment. It is crucial that policies on bullying and harassment are in place and well publicized. Employers are responsible for preventing bullying and harassment – they're legally liable for any harassment suffered by their employees. ACAS's publication *Bullying and harassment at work: a guide for managers and employers* offers practical advice to employers to help them prevent bullying and harassment and to deal with any cases that occur. It includes guidelines for the development of policies and procedures. Go to acas.org.uk and download *Bullying and harassment at work: a guide for managers and employers*.

In their 2015 report, *Seeking better solutions: tackling bullying and ill-treatment in Britain's workplaces*, ACAS report that 'experts and researchers are clear that relying on individuals to speak out on bullying is problematic. . .When it comes to bullying and ill-treatment. . .these behaviours are best prevented by means of organisation-wide strategies that focus proactively on ensuring worker wellbeing and fostering good workplace relations.'

Provide a Good Physical Work Environment

As well as feeling psychologically safe, employees need to feel physically safe and comfortable in their work settings. The physical work environment – noise levels, space, temperature, and light – can significantly affect staff wellbeing. Workplaces must be suitable for all who work in them, including workers with any kind of disability. Under the law, employers must make sure that their workplace complies with the Workplace Health, Safety and Welfare Regulations. These regulations – which cover a wide range of basic health, safety, and welfare issues – lay down minimum standards for workplaces and work in or near buildings. The regulations apply to most types of workplace except transport, construction sites, and domestic premises and cover issues such as space, temperature, cleanliness, lighting, ventilation, humidity, and welfare facilities, including access to drinking water.

The Health and Safety Executive's hse.gov.uk downloadable guide *Workplace health, safety and welfare: a short guide for managers* as well as other publications about health and safety are available to inform you.

4
How to Look After Your Wellbeing at Work

Between stimulus and response there is a space, in that space is our power to choose our response. In our response lies our growth and freedom. Everything can be taken from a man but one thing: the last of human freedoms – to choose one's attitude in any given set of circumstances, to choose one's own way.

Victor E. Frankl.
Auschwitz survivor and psychologist

To a large extent, our wellbeing and mental health at work is in our control; we each have the ability to deal with most situations, cope with difficulties and challenges, and bounce back. This ability is called resilience. Like everyone else, you have the potential to be resilient but it does require thought and effort on your part. In this chapter, we suggest a number of ways in which, whatever your role or position at work, whatever your skills, experience, and abilities, you can develop the psychological, social, and physical resources that will help you to manage pressure and minimize stress, maintain and improve your mental health and wellbeing at work. Of course, developing your resilience doesn't mean that you'll become impervious; if, as described in Chapter 1, pressure and demands are unrelenting, it can lead to burnout. Nonetheless, there's still plenty you can do to protect and strengthen yourself.

Establish and Maintain a Good Work–Life Balance

Creating a balance between working and not working is essential when it comes to your wellbeing. Sometimes it can feel like work is taking over your life. It's not just that you spend most of your day at work; even when you're not there, you're still thinking about it. And with constant access to the internet, email, and texts, it's easy to stay plugged in all day when you're at work and when you're away from it.

A healthy work–life balance – or to use another term; 'work–life harmony' – is about making sure that both your work interests and demands *and* your personal needs, interests, and priorities are being met. If you're continually working long hours with little time for anything else, the cumulative effect of neglecting aspects of your life that help you resist or manage mental and physical health problems – rest, physical activity, healthy eating, leisure activities, and friendships – can leave you vulnerable and be detrimental to your physical and mental wellbeing.

You can easily keep track of the hours you put in over a period of weeks or months. Each day, write down how many hours you've worked. Be aware, too, of the time you spend thinking or worrying about work when assessing your work–life balance; time spent thinking, worrying, or being anxious about work *is* work and a good indicator of work-related stress.

Think if you have let other aspects of your life slide beneath your feet – time with family and friends, time for leisure activities. Do you do less of the things you'd like or need to do than you used to, because of the time you spend working?

You need to set work hours for yourself and do everything in your power to stick to them. Here are a few ways to switch off and leave work behind:

Set a firm cut-off time. To get yourself away from work by, say 5 or 5.30 p.m., plan something; an activity or event for after work. It could be meeting up with a friend for a drink, a meal, a walk, a class, or to see a film. It could be an exercise class, or to get home and walk the dog or if you work from home, it could be stopping by a certain time in order to make dinner. How does this help? Because knowing you have something else to attend to creates a different obligation and can move you away from work.

Stop before you stop. Whatever time you decide you'll stop work each day, aim to stop your task-based work about 5–10 minutes before you actually leave. Set a timer or alarm (not something loud and harsh; try a mindfulness bell instead; it's gentler) to let you know that your closing routine is about to begin.

My way of finishing work is to do one last task that earlier in the afternoon, I'd chosen to be my last task of the day. I then tidy my workspace, take out my contact lenses and put on my glasses. And I'm good to go!

Karim. Social worker

Get closure; leave work at work. As part of your closing routine, before you leave work, empty your head. Simply write a note or email to yourself of any work-related things that are on your mind; tasks left to do and any concerns. It's hard to stop thinking about work, even after we've put it away for the day. Our brains are hard-wired to keep us thinking about our unfinished tasks until we've completed them. (It's what's known as the Zeigarnik Effect.)

While thinking about uncompleted tasks may prompt you to finish what you've started, it can leave you worried and stressed. There is, though, a simple mental short-cut you can take to stop worrying about unfinished work: simply writing down what needs doing the next day in order to complete specific tasks provides the same mental relief as actually completing the task. The following day, starting with a clear, prioritized to-do list also cuts down on the number of decisions you'll have to make early in the day. So, write it down, then shut the notebook, turn off your computer and walk away.

Make the commute less stressful. David Spencer, Professor of Economics and Political Economy at the University of Leeds, suggests that any time or effort spent working during your commute isn't worth it. 'The encroachment of work into commute time simply extends the length of the working day, for no extra pay', he says. Your commute time might be better spent doing something calming before and after work; a meditation app, a good audiobook, or podcast.

Use your legs. A 2017 study, *Commuting and Wellbeing*, by the University of the West of England found that active commuters didn't feel robbed of leisure time to the extent that others do, implying they view it as a beneficial use of time, getting exercise and relaxation. However, be aware that pollution spikes in the evenings, so if you can, take the less polluted, back street route home.

Give yourself a positive debrief. Write down three positive things that happened that day. Something, no matter how small, that you achieved, that you found of interest, you learnt, made you laugh, a positive interaction with someone else.

Set boundaries. If clients or colleagues think it's OK to call you at 8 p.m., they will. Set firm boundaries around when you are and aren't, available. If people are used to reaching you and getting a response at any time of day or night, tell them this will no longer be the case. Let them know by setting up an automatic message that replies to out-of-office emails that says something like 'Thank you for your email. My work hours are Monday–Friday, from 10 a.m.–6 p.m. I'll reply to your message as soon as possible.'

Of course, texting is based on different expectations; to send a text is to expect a rapid, even immediate reply. But still, you need to make it clear that you're not endlessly available for work queries outside working hours. Unless it's an emergency, as long as you do answer the next working day, people get to know that and trust that they will receive a reply – just not as quickly as they'd hoped. Unless your job specifically requires you to be on call 24/7, there's little that happens after 6 p.m. that can't wait until the morning.

Disconnect. Get used to being without your phone, tablet, or laptop. Give yourself a few hours to disconnect, otherwise you can find yourself in a state of permanent activity with little in the way of a rest or break when technology puts you somewhere that you're not. An activity that's completely different from what you do at work is a good way to get away from everyday pressures. Go hiking or cycling. (Take a phone but turn it off.) Play a sport. Do something creative, artistic, or musical. Whatever you enjoy doing. . .make sure you set aside time to do it. And do more of it more often!

Take a Proper Lunch Break

In 2016, after failing to take a lunch break for several weeks, Laura Archer decided to reclaim her lunch hour. She started to write a list of things she could do in her lunch break and was surprised to find that she'd come up with a list of 40 things. Was it, she wondered, possible to come up with 52 ideas – a different idea for each week of the year? Turns out it was. Laura separated the activities into four categories – Active, Sitting, Inside, and Outside. Some of the activities only need 20 minutes a day, others need a full 45–60 minutes. You can discover for yourself all of Laura's ideas in her book *Gone For Lunch. 52 things to do in your lunch break*.

But a lunch break doesn't have to mean a lunch hour. Even if you take 20 minutes away from your desk once or twice a week, it can make a positive difference to your mood.

In an interview in the *Evening Standard*, Laura Archer was asked what the main difference was that she had noticed in herself since she started taking lunch breaks:

> I didn't actually notice the positive effects of taking a lunch break until I hit a really busy period at work. For 3 months I didn't have the time to do more than rush to grab a sandwich. My mood became incredibly overcast and my attitude to my job plummeted. Everything felt grey when I looked back over my week. My energy levels crashed and with that my diet and my health. I'd be so exhausted by the end of the day that I'd

opt for a take-away or ready meal, and seek a lift from coffee, sweet snacks and alcohol. As soon as I was able to take a lunch break again, everything got better.

Asked what she does on those days you feel you really can't take a full break from your desk, Laura says that what she found to be most important is simply having time away from your computer and phone.

Our vision is so limited during the working day – we look straight ahead of us, whether it's at a computer or another person in a meeting. We rarely look further than a metre or two ahead. I go and sit by a window or in a park and look into the distance. It sounds mad, but you can feel your brain sighing in relief – your shoulders relax and your body takes a break from the tense positions we hold ourselves in when under time pressure.

If you're someone who struggles to take a lunch break, or eats at their desk, start by committing yourself to one or two days a week of taking your full lunch break.

Eat well. What you eat, and when you eat, can make a difference to how you feel at any point in the day. Taking care of yourself by eating healthily is simply a matter of making the healthy choices easier to choose and eat. Try and plan for mealtimes at work – bringing food from home or choosing healthy options when buying lunch. Avoid snacks which make your blood sugar rise and fall rapidly, such as sweets, cakes, biscuits, and sugary drinks. Instead, keep a ready supply of fruit/vegetables and snacks like mixed fruit and nuts.

Take a Holiday

Sometimes, it can be hard to take holidays and time off from work. You may feel that by taking time off, you're giving extra work to your workmates, or worry that your work won't be covered while you're away and that having a pile of work to come back to isn't worth taking time off. Perhaps you feel that you need to show extra commitment by being at work all the time. Or you worry that taking time off might affect a promotion or your career prospects.

If you're concerned about work left undone, as far as possible, delegate work to colleagues before you leave so you know you won't return to chaos. Don't feel guilty! Guilt is a feeling that you've done something wrong. But you've not done anything wrong by taking a break. Every employee in the UK has a basic entitlement of 5.6 weeks annual leave: that's 28 days every year for full-time workers and pro rata for part-time employees.

Paid holiday leave is not a favour granted by your employer, it's a legal entitlement to a break from work. It supports your wellbeing by giving you time to spend with family and friends and/or pursuing hobbies and interests. Or you could spend time off doing very little at all!

Try and plan periods of leave for the year so that you always have a break to look forward to. Plan a holiday with friends and family so you can't let them down by backing out. Commit yourself to a break by booking accommodation, flights, train or coach journeys in advance.

Flexible Working

Flexible working can help contribute towards a positive work–life balance. More and more people are working flexibly, at times and in locations that fit around their lives. Flexible working arrangements may include, for example:

- changing from full-time to part-time work;
- changing the part-time hours that you work, for example, from weekends to weekdays;
- changing working hours to fit in with, for example, school hours, or care arrangements;
- compressed hours, that is, working your usual hours in fewer days;
- flexitime, which allows you to fit your working hours around agreed core times;
- home working for part or all of the time;
- job sharing;
- term-time work, so you don't work during the school holidays.

Flexible working might already be available within your company, so do find out what's on offer before making a more formal request. After 26 weeks of continuous service, you have the right to make a formal request. It's a legal requirement that you write a letter or an email addressed to your employer, labelled as a 'statutory request', with the date clearly stated. Once submitted, your employer must respond within three months with a yes or no answer. If they refuse your request and you think it wasn't considered fairly, you'll be eligible to appeal against their decision.

Your request is more likely to be approved if you've taken into account their needs as well as your own. Explain how the changes will work for both you and your employer. This shows that you've put some real thought into the change, and can justify why it's a good idea. If your proposed changes could affect the business negatively, then your employer could have a good reason to say no. So, do address the possible difficulties, and suggest realistic ways to overcome them.

When I reduced my hours at work from working five to four days a week, I found that working less hours prompted me to focus more on each task; I stopped jumping from one thing to the next. I'd finish one thing before moving on to the next one, and by the end of the day found I was accomplishing more than trying to do one thing while thinking about two other things that needed doing.

I became more aware of how I was doing things and why I was doing them. I didn't feel any more stressed at work probably because I only thought about and did one thing at a time. And, of course, I had the extra day off to enjoy.

Joshua. Branch manager at a financial
services company

99

You can find out what you need to do by going to acas .org.uk/flexibleworking or Citizens Advice citizens advice.org.uk and look for their page on flexible working.

Manage Stressful Busy Periods at Work

It could be that your work–life balance is not a problem; the hours you work are manageable. What may be difficult is the pressure at work; the amount you have to do in the time you have. It's stress.

Stress is the feeling of being under too much mental or emotional pressure. It's the strain and distress that are caused as a result of being overloaded with pressure and demands. Stress can affect how you feel, think, behave, and how your body works. (See Chapter 1 for a more detailed description of stress – the signs and symptoms.) Different people find different events and situations more or less stressful than others. We each have events or situations – deadlines, delays, doing several things at once, catching up with what you haven't done and what you've yet to do, other people's needs and demands – that are particularly stressful to us. Most of us might be able to cope with one thing we find stressful but when they all mount up it can become a real struggle to cope. Feelings of stress overtake your mind and prevent you from thinking clearly.

Why is that? It helps to understand what's going on in your head; to know that it's all down to two specific areas of your brain: the amygdala and the neocortex. The neocortex part of your brain is responsible for thinking, remembering, rationalizing and reasoning. Focus and attention are primarily an activity of the neocortex. The problem is, when you become stressed, the amygdala is triggered and it overwhelms the neocortex. The amygdala in your brain is responsible for your emotions; emotions such as agitation, anxiety, frustration, which, when you're under pressure, can overwhelm your neocortex and so prevent you from thinking clearly, rationally and reasonably.

But some people thrive and rise to the challenge of lots to do; deadlines to meet and plans to reorganize. How come? Because they just stay with what's happening and what they're doing right now. They're completely focused. They don't allow the amygdala to take over but instead allow the pressure to motivate and energize them and they engage the neocortex; the thinking, reasoning part of the brain.

You can do the same.

You just need to calm down the emotional part of your brain and engage the rational reasoning part of your brain so that you can work out what practical things you can do to manage and reduce the stress. Here's how you can do that:

Accept it. Instead of stressing yourself out and filling your mind with what you haven't done and what else you've got to do, instead of telling yourself how unfair and difficult things are, recognize that there *is* only a certain amount of time available to get things done, or, if something has come up and forced you to change your plans, then recognize and accept that you're going to *have* to reorganize your day. Accept it. Stop allowing the amygdala to take over and waste your time and energy railing and resenting it. Accept that the shit *has* hit the fan.

Now breathe. Simply take two minutes to stop what you're doing and focus on breathing. A two-minute breathing space will help calm you down, collect and clarify your thoughts. It's not easy but if you *can* do that then you free up your brain to think more clearly and deliberately and you'll be more likely to find a way through.

Prioritize and plan. No matter how many times you hear it, it's still a truism; when there's lots to do and little time to do it in, you need to plan and prioritize. Even when – or especially when – things are urgent, you can still prioritize and plan what needs to be done. You simply need to work out what's really important and then work out what steps you'll need to take to get things done.

Look at everything you've got to do or could be done for a particular task; whatever it is that needs to be done by a certain time. Write it all down. Instead of letting it all swirl around your head, write it all down. Look through your list, decide what's important – what has to be done or what you really want to get done.

Before you do anything, work out what's important; what steps you need to take to meet that deadline. Now write them down in the order that you'll do them.

It's easier to get straight on to the next step if you've already planned what and how you are going to do it. It allows you to maintain a steady pace and keep the pace going. A step-by-step plan allows you to simply work consistently towards what it is you want to achieve; you'll know that at any one point in the hour or the day, you're clear about what you are going to work on.

Have realistic expectations and goals. Decide how much can realistically be done in an hour, a morning, a day, and so on. Set achievable targets. When you're under a lot of pressure it's easy to set yourself large targets that are unachievable. This can make you feel more overwhelmed because if you don't reach them, you can feel even more stressed. Setting small achievable goals can make you feel in control because as you achieve each step, you can see yourself making progress.

A good tip here: whatever it is you're hoping to get done, consider a half-size version. Compare your original version and the half-size version, and ask yourself which feels a better, more realistic goal.

Make some space; don't plan things close together, instead, leave room between activities and tasks. If, for example, you have a meeting, block out a 15-minute slot afterwards. This will give you time to decompress, and ensure you won't have to go through intense meetings back-to-back. Leaving space between activities and tasks makes your time more flexible; it gives you some time in case one thing takes longer than you planned or something urgent comes up. There will always be urgent tasks that you couldn't have foreseen; you can't always predict or avoid some issues and crises. That's why, just like having savings to deal with unexpected financial issues, it's a good idea to plan for some spare time – time in your day and week to handle unexpected issues, delays, and difficulties.

Manage your energy. Take your physical and mental focus and energy into account; think about your optimum times of the day. The optimum times are the times in the day when your physical and mental energy and concentration levels are at a maximum.

Some tasks such as writing bids and reports, filling in forms, need all your focus and concentration. However, it's not a good use of time and energy if you try to do these things at a time of day that doesn't work for you. Attempt a task when your mind is wandering or you're too tired to focus and you're unable to concentrate and the law of diminishing returns kicks in: each minute of effort produces fewer and fewer results. That's because trying to get something done at your least optimum time of day takes more and more effort, energy, and concentration with the result that things end up being done badly or not at all. Conversely, getting certain things done at your optimum time of day will take less effort and energy because it's easier to be present; to focus and concentrate on what's happening and what needs doing.

Identify what sort of jobs or activities you can only spend a short time on. Are you easily bored or distracted by some tasks? Probably best to plan to do them when your ability to focus is at its highest; at your optimum time of day.

Once you know which hours are *less* productive for you, you can plan and schedule easy, mundane tasks for those times. And, knowing which times of the day are not your most productive can help you stop feeling guilty because you know it just isn't the best time for you to get work done.

Work out what's the optimum amount of time you can focus on different tasks and activities. It may be that you're best doing things in short bursts, rather than one big stretch. So, that might mean that three sessions of 20 minutes' focused attention could be better than one long 60-minute slog. Try the 'short bursts' technique and see if it works for you.

Vary your activities. Balance interesting tasks with more mundane ones, and stressful tasks with those you find easier or can do more calmly.

Get started. Once you're clear about what you're going to do and when, get started. Do the first step. Give it your full attention. Once that one thing is done, go on to the next step. Give that your full attention too. Keep your mind focused on one step at a time. Tell yourself, 'This is what I'm going to do next' and then just focus on that one step you're taking.

With this focused step-by-step approach, you can be deliberate and purposeful, not rushed and random. You simply focus on what you're doing right now, at the present time, instead of getting stressed filling your mind with what you haven't done and what else you've got to do.

Breathe. If you *do* start thinking about what else you have to do, remind yourself you've already scheduled that in and pull yourself back to what you're doing. Pause, breathe, and pull yourself back. Tell yourself 'I have a plan. I can manage this'.

Slow down. If you find yourself speeding up, whatever you do next, slow it down by 20%, whether it's typing on a keyboard or digging a hole. Try slowing down by 20%. It feels strange but it really can help you be calm, focus on what you're doing and what's happening. Try it!

Be flexible. No matter how much you plan, challenges and setbacks happen. You then have to let go of your plans. And plan again.

Do take some breaks. No matter how little time you have in your day. Breaks give your mind space to digest, mentally process, and assimilate what's happening, what is working and what isn't, and to decide if you need to change anything.

Reflect. At the end of each day take time to reflect. Ask yourself what worked today and what didn't. Do the same at the end of each week too. For anything that didn't go well, ask yourself what you've learnt from that and what you might do differently, next time. Be aware too, that whenever you've finished something, it's easy to just move onto what needs to be done next and not acknowledge what you've just achieved. Even with small things like finishing a piece of work or making a decision, tell yourself 'well done'.

Quit while you're ahead. Use Ernest Hemingway's approach; 'I always worked until I had something done and I always stopped when I knew what was going to happen next. That way I could be sure of going on the next day.' Stopping while you're ahead is a good tactic: You know what you've done, you know exactly what you'll do next, and you'll likely feel OK about getting started again.

Stress: know your rights. The Health and Safety Executive say that, 'if you are feeling signs of stress at work, it is important to talk to someone, for example your manager. If you talk to them as soon as possible, it will give them the chance to help and stop the situation getting worse.'

What, though, if you feel you can't talk to your manager? In a recent survey by Mind, 30% of staff disagreed with the statement 'I would feel able to talk openly with my line manager if I was feeling stressed'.

Your employer has a legal duty to assess the risks to your health from stress at work and share the results of any risk assessment with you. So, do find out if a risk assessment has been done and also see what policies are in place at work to deal with stress.

If you feel unable to talk to your manager you can talk to one of the following, for advice and guidance:

- Your trade union representative
- ACAS
- An employee representative
- Your HR department
- An employee assistance programme/counselling service if your company has these, or
- Your GP.

Know Your Limits. Be Assertive; Say No!

Feeling overwhelmed and stressed doesn't mean you're incompetent and no good at your job. Many organizations try to make do with fewer staff, so there is more work to do for those of you that are there. One of the key resources for managing workplace stress – whether it's an unmanageable work–life balance, work overload, unreasonable or unrealistic demands – is the ability to say no.

You may worry that by refusing to do something or put up with something, others will get annoyed or upset or not take you seriously. You may be concerned that if you speak out you'll put your job at risk.

But saying nothing and suffering in silence is not going to make things better! The Mental Health Foundation recommends that 'when work demands are too high, you *must* speak up. This includes speaking up when work expectations and demands are too much. Employers need to be aware of where the pressures lie in order to address them.'

It is not only OK to set boundaries, it's necessary. Being able to turn other people down is a skill that will help you manage other people's requests, demands, and interruptions. Saying no to unimportant things – unnecessary meetings or extra work – means that you can say yes to important things; the things you want to do, that need doing, and that you like doing; the things that enable you to be productive. You'll need be assertive. Here's how:

- **Be clear about what you're being asked to do.** If you're not sure what you're being asked to do, ask for more information so that you're clear about what's involved. And if you're not sure whether you've got the time or ability, don't be afraid to ask for time to think about it before you commit yourself. Say when you'll get back to the person asking and give a definite time you'll get back with an answer. If the other person says they need an answer immediately (they have a right to do this) then rather than say yes and regret it later, it's best if you say no right now.

- **Be honest, clear, and succinct.** If you're unwilling or simply unable to do what's been asked of you, you'll need to say no. You'll need to be clear and direct; no waffling, excuses, or elaborate explanations.
- **Give just one reason.** Don't blame someone or something else, just be honest. You only need one genuine reason for saying no. One reason is always enough. Just say what it is. Rather than say 'I'm sorry, I would do it but I've got so much on; I can hardly think straight and I'm so behind with everything. I hope you don't mind too much. Isn't there someone else that can do it? Sorry.' Say 'I'm sorry, I'm not going to be able to. . .' and then give your reason.
- **Acknowledge the other person's response but stand your ground.** Once you've said what you've got to say, say no more. Just listen to the other person's response. Then acknowledge their response but stand firm. For example 'I understand you need someone to. . . (acknowledging their response) but. . .I'm not going to be able to do it.' (standing your ground).
- **Negotiate and compromise.** You might, though, decide to negotiate or compromise with the other person. For example, you might say 'I could ask someone else if they'd be prepared to. . .' Or 'I could maybe do what you've asked if you're happy for me to drop a couple of other tasks and focus on this instead.' Or 'I could get it done by a

later date' or 'I can't do that, but I can. . .' If you do choose to negotiate or compromise, bend as far as you can, but no further. Know what your limits are and stand your ground.

Be Assertive About What You Want

Your job description should clearly and specifically describe the responsibilities for your position.

If, though, you are now performing duties that are too challenging, too easy or otherwise incorrectly assigned, you'll need to assert yourself and discuss the issue with your manager. Before you meet, write down the tasks and duties you've been doing recently but that are not in your job description. Bring the list and a copy of your job description to your meeting. Explain your current workload, and the duties that you think are beyond your job description and/or level of responsibility, knowledge, or skill.

Calmly explain what the problem is. If, for example you were finding it difficult to manage an increased workload, you might say: 'This assignment requires a lot of research, which is taking up a lot of my time each day,' or 'Now that I'm managing a team, I'm spending more time planning, as well as doing my usual day-to-day work.'

Then, offer one or two ideas for addressing the issue. Or, ask what they'd suggest. For example: 'Which of these is most important? And how would you prioritize the rest?' Don't agree on the spot to anything new if you're unsure whether you can deliver. Simply say you'll need some time to think about it and say when you'll get back to them. Whatever the outcome, do get it in writing – even just an email to confirm what you believe has been agreed.

Knowing your limits is an essential part of working with other people. For two reasons. Firstly, because it helps you to know when to say no to other people's requests and demands. Secondly, knowing your limits means that you know when something is beyond you and you need to ask others for their help.

Get Help with Your Work

Mind's publication *How to Implement the Thriving at Work Mental Health Standards in Your Workplace* recognizes that as much as human resources, senior leaders and line managers all have key roles and responsibilities for promoting wellbeing and good mental health at work, employees themselves are *'responsible for accessing support when they need it and raising any concerns with their line manager, HR or occupational health.'*

If you're feeling swamped, you need to let others know. Perhaps colleagues can take something off your plate or work with you on something. You'll need to talk with your manager about this. Perhaps, though, you think that asking for help means you're admitting you're inadequate in some way; you don't want anyone to see that you're struggling, you want people to think that you're in control and can handle things. But the thing is, you get in your own way if you don't ask for help. Asking for help doesn't say something negative about you. Quite the opposite – it shows that you know that trying to do everything yourself is not the best use of your time, skills, or energy; it can leave you feeling overwhelmed and stressed and then you can't do anything properly.

Don't use up your time and energy doing tasks that others may have the time and/or ability to do! Get things done properly and more easily; find someone who's got the time or is good at what you need to learn or get done and then ask for their help and guidance. Know that asking for some help with understanding something at work, for example, acknowledges the other person's knowledge and abilities. And be aware that if the problem is an aspect of a team project, you're letting other people down by *not* seeking help; you're not the only one affected if you refuse to seek help!

Asking for help – or simply delegating some tasks and chores – gives you more time to focus on what's most important, useful or necessary. It can free you up to focus on what you – and maybe only you – can do well. So, change your beliefs and expectations. Tell yourself 'I can get things done well if I ask someone else to help me.' Tell yourself that asking for help is less embarrassing than failing at whatever you're finding difficult to cope with.

If you need others to help, to give ideas, to solve problems with you, don't hesitate to draw them in. If you're in a position of authority, you can delegate; give a particular job, task, or duty to someone else so that they do it for you. Otherwise, you simply ask. Here's how:

Know what, exactly, you want help with and what needs doing. The clearer you are about what you want help with, the better you can explain it to someone else. People who successfully delegate and get help are clear about what they want. They make it easy for others to understand what needs doing, how, and by when.

Ask directly. Don't drop hints. Don't say 'God this is difficult' or 'I've got so much to do'. Don't waffle or apologize for needing help. Don't say 'I know you're really busy, so only if you have time. . .only if you want to. . .'. Instead, just tell the other person what you're trying to achieve and what you'd like them to do. Simply say 'I need help with. . . Would you be able to. . .show me/do it for me/get it for me?' This way, the person is clear about what, how, and when to help you.

Make it easy for someone to help you. Ask the right person for their help – someone who has the ability, knowledge, or time. Unless you've got plenty of time to show someone or train them to do something that's unfamiliar to them, make sure that what you ask them to do matches their skills and ability.

However, don't always assume you know what other people can do. Even if those you ask can't help you directly, they might know someone who can help, they might have some ideas or solutions or some other information that would help you. Until you ask, you don't know who or what other people know or can do!

Delegate, don't dump. Sometimes, what passes for delegation, for the other person, feels like they've been dumped on; that you've just offloaded work onto them without any thought or consideration for their situation. Does the other person actually have time to take on more work? Will delegating a job to them mean that they will need to reshuffle their current commitments? If so, what do they think and how do they feel about that? What are their concerns? Ask them. Include people in the delegation process. If possible, be flexible. Offer options and negotiate.

Follow-up. If you ask someone to do something for you, be clear about what needs doing but let them determine the process. Be available to answer questions but don't micro manage; focus on the end result rather than detailing exactly how the work should be done. Your way is not necessarily the only way or even the best way! Let people do things their own way.

Say thank you. Finally, of course, make sure you express your appreciation. Whether you're saying thanks to a colleague who has made you a cup of coffee or letting someone know how grateful you are that they helped you on a difficult project or they sorted out an IT problem for you, gratitude goes a long way to developing good working relationships.

Build Positive Relationships with Others

Working supportively and cooperatively with others is key to supporting your wellbeing and mental health at work. Connecting with others is not just for difficult or busy periods at work though. Other people can be a source of support in a number of situations and can make being at work more enjoyable.

- Be welcoming to new members of staff. Remember what it was like when you were new. Without being overbearing, share the knowledge, the lessons, the experiences, and the skills you've accumulated.
- Aim to be sociable with your co-workers. When you take a break, for example, instead of looking at your phone, engage with your colleagues. Find common ground. You won't always have lots in common with all your colleagues, but finding something that you both like – such as a sports team, TV programme, or hobby – can give you something positive to talk about and help build good relationships.
- Be nice. You can choose to be there or not for colleagues. While it's important not to take on too much when you've already got a lot to do, helping others doesn't have to involve a lot of time or effort. Even small things like a kind word or friendly smile can make a difference to someone's day. Ask how someone's weekend was; show interest and ask questions about what they tell you. Carry out random acts of kindness; occasionally

bring in cake or fresh fruit, offer to make tea or coffee for others.

- Get involved with or organize lunchtime events; a walk or a swim for example. Learn something new with colleagues; learn how to play chess or to knit for example. Now and again, do something after work; bowling, a dance class, a meal out, etc.

I really enjoy running and the physical and mental health benefits that it brings so I started a running group at work. Our weekly run brings together colleagues of all running abilities from across company. The support and camaraderie between colleagues means that each run ends with everyone feeling good – no matter how hard the run! We sometimes enter marathons and half marathons together and raise money for a good cause.

Michael. Call centre worker

- Aim to be inclusive; enable others to be involved in what you're doing.
- Volunteer together – you could, for example, give blood in your lunch hour blood.co.uk.
- Do It do-it.org/news/using-your-work-volunteer-days and Time Bank (go to timebank.org.uk and search for employee volunteering) can help you find suitable opportunities for a one-off team project or a personalized programme for your workplace.
- Find out if your line of work has a professional association. If, for example, you are a company

secretary or administrator, membership of the Institute of Chartered Secretaries and Administrators icsa.org.uk gives you access to training and opportunities to meet other in your profession. If you are a forester, membership of charteredforesters .org gives you access to their peer network and knowledge base. Professional associations, their events, and activities give you opportunities to meet and talk with others about the same workplace issues, the ups and downs.

- Make friends with trusted supportive colleagues with whom you can mutually discuss thoughts and feelings about work. If you are open about how you feel at work, especially if you are a leader, it can encourage others to do the same. Don't, though, let things turn into a moan fest.
- Steer clear of the moaners and the gossips. (People often use gossip as a way of bonding but it can cause conflict, so try to avoid getting involved). Hanging out with negative-minded people who do nothing but complain will only drag you down and drain your energy; their misery, criticism, and complaining can overwhelm you. Of course, it's not always possible or practical to switch off from negative people or remove yourself from them completely, but you can be aware of the effect their negativity is having on you and, as much as possible, limit the amount of time you spend around them. And when you do encounter them, afterwards, take some time to re-energize yourself.
- Seek out and spend more time with positive colleagues. Positive people are likely to respond

to you in positive ways and so make you think positively about yourself, your work, and the world around you.

Even though there are things you can do to build positive relationships with others, you're not always going to get on with everyone. Work politics can be a real challenge. So can having a difficult relationship with your colleagues or a manager; it can be stressful, and make work harder to manage. In fact, poor relationships at work can be really harmful when they are characterized by bullying and harassment.

Dealing with Bullying and Harassment

While the closely related concept of harassment is grounded in legal definition (in the Equality Act 2010 and other legislation) and has associated legal protections and recourse, there is no standard definition of what is considered to be an act of bullying. Ideas of what constitutes bullying behaviour can vary widely according to context and the perceptions of the people involved: what may be considered, for example, reasonable behaviour by one person may be experienced as bullying by another. The options for resolution can also be unclear.

Bullying is, as defined by ACAS, 'offensive, intimidating, malicious or insulting behaviour, an abuse or misuse of power through means that undermine, humiliate, denigrate or injure the recipient'. Bullying can happen to anyone.

By law, it is harassment when bullying or unwanted behaviour relates to any of the following (known as 'protected characteristics'): a person's age, their race, disability, gender reassignment, pregnancy and maternity, religion or belief, sex, or sexual orientation.

Harassment as defined in the Equality Act 2010 is: 'Unwanted conduct related to a relevant protected characteristic, which has the purpose or effect of violating an individual's dignity or creating an intimidating, hostile, degrading, humiliating or offensive environment for that individual.'

If you're being bullied then you may well feel very upset; anxious and frightened, ashamed, or embarrassed. You may feel angry and frustrated. You mustn't try and pacify or ingratiate yourself with them, but you *must* do something. The bully will not go away. Staying silent and telling no-one will only isolate you while at the same time empowering the bully, so you must get some help and support. Don't suffer in silence; there *is* help out there.

To start with, find out if your employer has a policy on bullying. The policy should outline how to address the problem and what the grievance procedure is. If you're not ready or feel unable to talk to someone at work about it, ACAS have advice on their website acas.org.uk (search for Bullying and Harassment at Work – a Guide for Employees). ACAS also have a helpline that can provide you with advice on what to do if you're being bullied at work; you can find the phone number on their website. Citizens Advice citizensadvice.org.uk can also provide information and advice. Go to their website and search for 'If you're being harassed or bullied at work'.

If you're being bullied and nothing changes for the better, or you do not feel as if you can take action, you may decide that leaving your job is the best option for your wellbeing and mental health.

By leaving, you regain control; you take away the opportunity for the bully to behave like this towards you. Being bullied and trying to manage being bullied is highly stressful. Ask yourself what's most important? Is it that you don't want to let the bully 'win'? Is that the most important issue? Rather than think in terms of one of you winning or losing, it's far better to think about keeping yourself safe and sane. Yes, you might have to walk away from a good job and financial stability, but focus on the positive; that you've left that person behind. Once you left, you can put your energy into finding a new job instead of spending your energy trying to please, pacify, or avoid the bully.

If you do want to think in terms of who's won and who's lost – know that if you take control and walk away – you have won. You *can* manage to find a new job or somewhere to live. What you can't manage is the bully. So refuse to allow your life to be wrecked and get out!

Wellness Action Plans

In Chapter 5 we explain how, if you are currently experiencing a mental health problem, a Wellness Action Plan

(WAP) can help you map out what needs to be in place for you to manage your mental health at work.

A WAP is something anyone can make use of – whether you have a mental health problem or not – to help you identify what supports your wellbeing at work. (Or if you work remotely or are a lone worker.) A WAP can get you thinking about:

- what situations at work can trigger stress at work
- what you can do for yourself to help manage stress at work
- what your manager can do to proactively support your wellbeing at work.

By completing a Wellness Action Plan, you will have thought through what does and doesn't work for you in terms of managing your wellbeing, what you can do to further improve your wellbeing. You can find out more about WAPS and get a free template at Mind's website. Search for 'Guide for Employees. Wellness Action Plans'.

Break up Sitting Time; Get Moving

Many of us take a train, bus or car for our commute to and from work. We spend hours at a desk, return home, and then slouch on the sofa for the evening. And we do it all sitting down.

In 2018, the World Health Organization listed inactivity as the fourth biggest risk factor for global adult mortality. Even if you do the recommended 150 minutes (in bouts of 10 minutes or more) of moderate aerobic exercise through the week (be it a run, a gym session or a brisk walk) if you spend long periods of every day sitting down, you're still classed as 'sedentary' and at risk of health problems. How come? Well, quite simply, sitting for long periods appears to slow the metabolism – which affects our ability to regulate blood sugar and blood pressure, and break down body fat – and may cause weaker muscles and bones. If there is little muscle activity it's as though your body is 'shutting down' when you're sitting.

The link between ill-health and sitting first emerged in the 1950s, when researchers found London bus drivers were twice as likely to have heart attacks as their bus conductor colleagues. More recently, a comprehensive review of studies on sedentary behaviour carried out by researchers from Loughborough University and the University of Leicester has linked sitting for lengthy periods with a range of health problems including an increased risk of heart disease, obesity, diabetes, and cancer.

But if sitting is the problem, could standing be the solution? Apparently not. Whether you sit or stand, it's being in one position that's the problem. You need to move more; take frequent breaks that involve moving.

The UK's 2016 government publication *Health Matters: Getting every adult active everyday* recommends that we should break up long periods of sitting time with short bouts of activity every 30 minutes. 'As well as being physically active, all adults are advised to minimise the time spent being sedentary (sitting) for extended periods. Even among individuals who are active at the recommended levels, spending large amounts of time sedentary increases the risk of adverse health outcomes.' It goes on to suggest that we should reduce the amount of time we sit during our working day by taking regular time *not* sitting during work and finding ways to break up sedentary time.

As Professor David Dunstan of the Baker IDI Heart and Diabetes Institute Melbourne, Australia says: 'Breaking up sitting time engages your muscles and bones, and gives all our bodily functions a boost – a bit like revving a car's engine.'

So if your work involves sitting or standing for long periods, how you can be more active? Here are a few ideas for making your working day more active.

Set a reminder. To help you get into the habit of moving more, use an app or phone reminder to prompt you to move around for a couple of minutes every 30–60 minutes.

Walk instead of calling or emailing. Pretend it's the 1990s! Instead of emailing, texting, or messaging a colleague across the room, walk over to their desk and talk with them face to face. Put your printer and your rubbish bin on the other side of the room so you have to get up to use them. Take phone calls standing up. And use the stairs, not the lift.

Turn waiting time into moving time. Waiting to use the photocopier, or for colleagues to vacate the meeting room you've booked? Don't stand there twiddling your thumbs. Take a stroll instead.

Stretch. Stand up to stretch out your chest and extend your spine to reverse the hunched position of sitting. As well as moving around, improve your posture. Activities that can help your posture include yoga, Tai Chi, Qigong, Pilates, and the Alexander Technique.

Drink more water. But don't have a bottle by your desk so you can sip throughout the day. Instead, leave it in the staff kitchen or somewhere else so that you have to get up and walk to every hour or so. Don't keep food next to you either; put it somewhere that you have to get up and go to. And use the toilets furthest away from your desk.

Volunteer for the coffee run. Go out and get your coffee, tea, or smoothie instead of letting someone else pick one up for you. Try and get in a 15-minute walk at lunch. Find a new sandwich shop that's further away from the one you usually use. And find new places to eat outside. See your lunchtime as a time to get moving and to enjoy your food, not a time to stuff something from the nearest food shop down your neck.

Organize walking meetings. Not only does it get you out of your chair, but it could be a good way to make sure meetings are more efficient and don't drag on unnecessarily.

Not everyone is able to get moving in this way if they have mobility problems. Matthew McCarthy, a researcher at University of Leicester Department of Cardiovascular Sciences, suggests that 'completing short bursts of upper body activities using resistance bands or table-top arm cranks' may be a way to activate your muscles and get moving.

If you have mobility problems, a physical condition, or find it difficult spending time out of a chair, the NHS website has activity routines you can try while sitting down and Disability Rights UK disabilityrightsuk.org/doing-sport-differently provides information about exercises you might be able to do. Also, take a look at bbc.co.uk/sport/get-inspired/23196217 for ideas about sports activities for people with disabilities.

As well as moving around every 30–60 minutes there's other things you can do to make your working day more active:

Walk, run, or cycle at least part of the way to and from work. If you can bike, walk, or even run to work, this can be an excellent way to fit more activity into your day. Even if you don't live close enough to your workplace to be able to do this, you can still find ways to make at least part of your journey more active. Get the train part of the way and ride the rest, get off the bus a few stops early and walk, or park your car a kilometre or two away or find the furthest car park space from your workplace building to park your car.

Start an office fitness challenge. Get your colleagues involved and make it a challenge to be more active together. As well as the physical health benefits, regular bouts of activity can help boost productivity. When you're moving, you are also increasing blood flow to the brain, which can help you stay alert and on top of things.

Make the Best of a Bad Job; Make Your Job Work for You

What if you'd like to leave your job, but for whatever reason, right now, you can't quit? What can you do to help make your time at work more bearable? There are still steps you can take to improve your situation.

Think positive. Rather than spend your time thinking how crap the job is – how boring or stressful it is – or how incompetent your manager is and/or how incompetent your colleagues are, be aware that when negative thoughts take control, they limit your ability to see opportunities for positive action. Stop with the negativity and instead, if you can't leave, start by looking for the positive aspects of your job. Perhaps your job is close to home and so you have a short journey to work? Is your commute a long one but you get to listen to the radio in the car or you get to read, listen to, or watch something on your laptop or tablet on the train?

Change your hours. As well as being aware of the positive aspects of your job, look for those aspects of the job that you *can* control. Instead of making yourself miserable railing against the things you can't change, look to see what you *can* change. Perhaps you have the sort of job where you could negotiate a day working from home? (See page 98 on Flexible Working.) Or maybe you could reduce your hours? If you think you could manage on less money, asking to reduce your hours can be an effective way to spend less time working somewhere that you're unhappy and give you more time and space to pursue interests outside of your job. You'll feel less defined by the job; it won't be such a dominant part of your life. Working fewer hours could also free you up to look for other jobs and attend interviews.

Set yourself a challenge. Choose an aspect of your job that is particularly onerous; difficult, monotonous, or boring. Then set yourself a challenge to make it less difficult, monotonous, or boring. Maybe you have a job where you often have to listen to other people's complaints? Take it on as a challenge; make it your goal to become really good at managing and resolving customer complaints.

Is there something that interests you; that you feel strongly about that you could bring into your work? Perhaps, for example, you'd like your work to have more social impact?

Here's what Ali did:

> I got in touch with local charities and community groups to discuss ways that our company could collaborate with them to provide services to help a client group that was completely

different from our main client group. Not only did I start enjoying my job more, it also gave me the kind of experience I wanted for the work I knew that I really wanted to do in future.

Maybe you could take the lead on initiating changes and improvements at work; a more comfortable working environment, or more efficient methods and procedures, or a flexible working policy? If you're feeling unfulfilled and unhappy, finding the motivation to take the lead on something probably isn't going to feel like the obvious and enjoyable thing to do. But it does provide you with some meaning and purpose in your working week and it'll give you an extra skill for your next job.

Take charge of your own professional and personal development. Just because you're not able to leave your job right now doesn't mean you can't start working towards the next one. What would you like to do in your next job – is there a skill you'll need that you can develop in this job?

Find out about training already offered at work. Find out too about other training, courses, and workshops relevant to your job and ask if you can attend a training or if an outside trainer can come in and deliver training to you and other colleagues.

But if you can't develop new skills and challenges related to your work, then look for other ways you can learn new skills. Sal, for example, was saving to travel in South America for six months. He had a night job stacking shelves at a supermarket. The work was boring, dull, and repetitive. But he downloaded a language course so that while he was stacking shelves, he learnt Spanish.

You can learn new skills – retrain, study – in your lunchtime, on your commute, in the evenings, or at the weekend. Greta, for example, decided to learn how to code.

I knew it would be a useful skill, something that I could do freelance in future and it would enable me to work on my own terms. I signed up to two courses: one online and one at a local adult learning centre. I've enjoyed learning how to code. Now, in all the boring meetings at work, instead of getting wound up thinking what a waste of time it all is, I'm planning my next website or solving a programming problem in my head. Having something different and enjoyable to focus on has helped me to be happier.

5
Manage Your Mental Health at Work

The advice I'd give to somebody that's silently struggling is, you don't have to live that way. You don't have to struggle in silence. You can be un-silent. You can live well with a mental health condition, as long as you open up to somebody about it, because it's really important you share your experience with people so that you can get the help that you need.

Demi Lavato

If you've been diagnosed with a mental illness or are experiencing mental health problems you will need to know how best to manage and cope at work.

There are three clear areas to think about:

1. Proactive planning: identifying what you can do to avoid episodes of ill-health.
2. Maintenance: identifying what will assist you to stay well.

3. Risk management, crisis and recovery planning: putting systems into place so that you know who to go to and where to go if you are at risk.

1. Proactive Planning: Identifying What You Can Do to Avoid Episodes of Ill-health

Thinking about what you can do to avoid an episode of ill-health starts with knowing what could set off or trigger a decline; you have to be prepared to be proactive in understanding what may prevent a relapse and be willing to seek support. Just as you would expect to get advice and support and be proactive in managing a physical illness, a mental illness requires the same approach. A person with diabetes, for example, has to be aware of the warning signs of hyperglycaemia and hypoglycemia: learn what they can and cannot eat, how to manage blood sugars, the impact of stress, the impact on insulin levels of an increase in physical activity, and so on.

So, with mental health illness, you need to be alert to the warning signs; to the events and circumstances that could trigger a decline in your mental health and how to manage the symptoms. It may be, for example, that if you suffer from anxiety, an overload of work and looming deadlines can be a trigger which then triggers difficulties such a sleep problem, which then makes you less able to cope with other stressors at work and home and leads to a downward spiral. For someone else, it might be that a period of bad weather and commuting delays gets you down and it only takes a couple of other difficulties to occur to trigger a bout of depression.

If, for example, your manager has told you that you have made a mistake at work, the negative narrative you tell yourself that you 'always get it wrong' may kick start you into worrying about making another mistake. Worry about it then makes you stressed and before you know it, you're in a cycle of worry and stress.

Whatever your triggers, recognizing them is an important first step. Keeping a diary can be helpful. Being more aware of your triggers and the associated negative, unhelpful thoughts that you attach to particular events and experiences allows you to see if there are patterns or themes occurring.

Case Studies

Kate kept a thought diary for a couple of weeks. 'Each day, I wrote about events as they happened and the thoughts I attached to situations and events. For example when I missed a deadline at work, I found myself thinking "Why does this always happen to me?" I also wrote about upcoming events. I wrote down my self-talk about telling my parents I didn't want them to visit this weekend as I wanted to spend the weekend with my boys. I wrote down my thoughts about meeting a friend for lunch and I also wrote down my thoughts and self-talk about an upcoming meeting with my manager.

I was surprised at just how often I attached negative thoughts to all these events. For example, even though my manager and I have a good working relationship, when she said she wanted to meet with me about a project – even though I had done it well and completed in good time – I worried; I started thinking "I just know she's going to say I've done something wrong."

Keeping a track of my thoughts helped me identify patterns in my thinking, to understand how I see myself, other people, situations and events. I realise that so often, I jump to conclusions; I catastrophise and think I "know" what other people will be thinking.'

Nick also kept a thinking diary. He realized the negative things he said most often to himself were usually along the same lines. He called them his 'negative stories'. They included the 'my work colleagues are better than me' story and the 'I don't get things done well enough' story. He discovered he had much the same 'stories' most of the time, which helped him realize the fact that they had become habits; habitual ways of thinking, not necessarily truthful ways of thinking.

Like Nick and Kate, if you keep a diary of events and associated thoughts and feelings, you can begin to identify the sorts of things that trigger difficult, upsetting thoughts. You may not consciously be aware of your self-talk and how your subconscious mind is taking it all in and accepting what you tell yourself, but once you're more aware of your negative self-talk you can start to do something about it.

When you are feeling anxious or depressed, notice your thoughts. Are they negative and judgemental?

Can you identify what may have triggered these unhelpful thoughts and reactions? Write it down.

As well as being a useful way to identify triggers and negative thought patterns, you can use a thought diary to write about the positive, helpful ways you can manage. Over time, you may then see your progress in moving through the difficulties.

2. Maintenance: Identifying What Will Help You Stay Well

Once you can identify and recognize what sort of circumstances and events could trigger a downturn in your mental health, you can start thinking about what can be put in place to assist you in staying well. Although you can identify for yourself the sort of things you can do (and there are a range of ideas and suggestions later in this chapter), your employer may be obliged to work with you to make what are known as 'reasonable adjustments' to your job or workplace to accommodate your needs and so enable you to be at work.

Support from Your Employer

If a person has a disability, reasonable adjustments are changes to their work and/or work environment that allow them to work safely and productively.

You may not think of yourself as a 'disabled person'. But if you have a mental illness, you may be affected by it in such a way as to be considered, in law, disabled (Equality Act 2010). Employers must provide reasonable adjustments to people who are eligible, including people with a mental illness such as schizophrenia, bipolar disorder, or depression.

Identifying the right changes at work for you now, and in the future, can reduce the impact of your health condition on your ability to work, and ensure you are getting the right support.

Any changes you ask for have to be reasonable, and you have to show that you are at a substantial disadvantage compared with other people because of your mental health problem. If changes are reasonable for your workplace to make, then it must make them.

The physical environment, your work routine, and workload are all aspects of your job where 'reasonable adjustments' can be made. Often the adjustments people might need are easy to implement and cost little if anything at all. For example, flexible working hours to allow for appointments with your GP or therapist. Or if symptoms become overwhelming or threaten to trigger difficulties, to be able to leave the workplace for a break if you need some time out. It might be that for you a reasonable adjustment would be to work from home on some days or on a regular basis. Or, if you are negatively affected by noise, moving to a quieter work area could be helpful.

If you are returning to work after a period of ill-health and have taken sick leave, a phased return to work, a job redesign, or redeployment may be considered as reasonable adjustments.

If you disclosed your mental health history at interview, your manager or Human Resources department may introduce the subject of adjustments when you first start working in your new job. Do, though, familiarize yourself with your legal rights regarding your health and any policies – including disability, support arrangements, sickness, and absence policies – before or immediately on starting work at the organization.

Even when you are entitled to workplace adjustments there are still limitations to what you can ask for. Employers do have a duty to provide 'reasonable adjustments', but this does depend on the type and size of organization and employer they are.

The mental health charity Rethink Mental Illness has a guide to your rights at work if you have a mental illness. Go to rethink.org and search for 'What's Reasonable at Work?'

If the help you need to be in work is not covered by your employer making reasonable adjustments, you may be able to get help from Access to Work. The UK Government's Access to Work scheme gov.uk/access-to-work aims to help more people with a physical or mental health disability to start or stay in work. The Access to Work Mental Health Support Service, delivered by 'Remploy' remploy.co.uk is available at no charge to any employees with depression, anxiety, stress, or other mental health issues affecting their work.

They can help provide:

- Tailored work-focused mental health support for nine months
- Suitable coping strategies
- A support plan to keep you in, or return to, work
- Ideas for workplace adjustments to help you fulfil your role
- Practical advice to support those with a mental health condition.

To be eligible for this service, individuals need to be in permanent or temporary employment and have a mental health condition (diagnosed or undiagnosed) that has resulted in workplace absence, or is causing difficulties to remain in work.

Supporting Yourself to Stay Well at Work

Although there are adjustments that can be made at work to help you manage your mental health and stay on top of things, there's a lot you can do for yourself to manage your mental health and keep well; to foster habits and routines to help build your resilience.

Breathe! If at any point in the day, feelings seem to be overwhelming you, mindful breathing can help focus your mind; reduce racing thoughts, heart rate, and blood pressure and help you feel more calm.

It's useful to know, though, that there's a difference between getting het up and calming back down. The difference is in the timing. The physical changes – rapid heartbeat, fast shallow breathing, and so on – all happen very quickly. But it takes longer for your body to 'come down'. Although it does take a while for the body to respond to a calming response, you *can* make it happen.

There's a range of breathing techniques that can help. Here's a couple you could try.

Count Your Breathing; Pranayama

- Empty your lungs of air; breathe out.
- Breathe in through your nose to the count of 4.
- Hold your breath for a count of 7.
- Slowly exhale through your mouth to the count of 8.
- Repeat the cycle up to 5 times, or until you feel calmer.

Feel Your Breathing

Feel your breathing. Place one hand on your chest and feel your breath moving into and out of your body. Notice the natural rhythm. Be aware of the coolness of the air as you breathe in and the warmth of the air leaving you as you exhale.

Concentrating on your breathing does two things: as well as slowing everything down – your rapid heartbeat and your racing thoughts – it can distract your mind and give it something helpful to think about. It's mindful; when you focus on your breathing you are focusing on something that is happening now, in the present. It helps to anchor or ground you. Managing your breathing also has the benefit of being a simple thing you can do anywhere, any time.

Get active. Exercise can have a powerful effect on your mental wellbeing. Our physical health and mental health are closely linked; physical activity can be beneficial for your mental health and wellbeing too. The benefits can be immediate. When you're physically active, your brain releases endorphins – the 'feel good' hormones – which can calm you, reduce feelings of anxiety and stress, and lift your mood. Physical activity helps to break up racing or intrusive thoughts; being physically active can give your brain something other than your worries to focus on, leaving you less stressed and calmer.

If you can bike, walk, or even run to work, this can be an excellent way to fit more activity into your day. Even if you don't live close enough to your workplace to be able to do this, you can still find ways to make at least part of your journey more active. Get the train part of the way and ride the rest, get off the bus a few stops early and walk, or park your car a kilometre or two away or find the furthest car park space from your workplace building to park your car.

At lunchtime, try to break away from your work, even if it's just a 15-minute walk; over a week it will soon mount up. (See Chapter 5 pages 122–127 for advice about breaking up sitting time.)

The NHS website nhs.uk/live-well/exercise/ provides guidelines for the amount of activity you need to be doing. Their website also suggests ways you can be more active. Go to nhs.uk/live-well/exercise/get-active-your-way/ and nhs.uk/live-well/exercise/free-fitness-ideas/.

Mind's initiative Get Set to Go helps people across England and Wales with mental health issues find the physical activity that's right for them so that they are able to enjoy the physical, social, and mental benefits of being active. Go to mind.org.uk and search for 'Get Set to GO'.

If you have mobility problems, a physical condition, or find it difficult spending time out of a chair, the NHS website has activity routines you can try while sitting down, and Disability Rights UK disabilityrightsuk.org/ doing-sport-differently provides information about exercises you might be able to do. Also, take a look at bbc.co.uk/sport/get-inspired/23196217 for ideas about sports activities for people with disabilities.

Eat well. What we eat and our eating patterns can have an impact on our health and wellbeing, both mentally and physically. Eating regularly and having a balanced diet can contribute to maintaining and improving your mood; can give you more energy and contribute to clearer thinking.

If you are unsure of the extent to which you're eating a healthy balanced diet, try keeping an eating diary – write down everything you eat in a week and then go to the NHS website nhs.uk/live-well/eat-well/ to see how your diet compares and what changes you could make.

Stay hydrated. If you are feeling thirsty, it may be that you are already slightly dehydrated. The recommendation is to drink 2 litres of fluid per day. Water is the ideal. If it is particularly hot or you are planning exercise, you may need to drink more. A note of caution – drinking 2 litres of fluid is good overall advice; if you have a known cardiac issue, check with your GP for guidance regarding fluid intake.

Avoid caffeine and alcohol, particularly when you're feeling anxious or depressed. In the long term it can make you feel worse.

Alcohol and recreational drugs can both cause depression. Although you might initially use them to make yourself feel better, or to distract yourself, they can make you feel worse overall.

Mind

If you think you may be drinking because it helps you to relax after a day at work, do be aware that, as well as interrupting sleep patterns, drinking more than the recommended units will eventually be detrimental to your health (men and women are advised not to drink more than 14 units a week. 14 units is 6 pints of 4% beer or 6 glasses of 13% wine). Look for healthier ways to relax; physical activity – a walk, run, or swim – a hot bath, meditation, a good book, time with family, friends, or a pet, for example.

If you suffer with anxiety, caffeine can contribute to feeling even more stressed; it can lead to palpitations and feeling too speedy. Starting the day with a coffee can be a good 'pick me up' but if you are having 3 to 4 coffees a day then it may contribute to stress during the day and an inability to relax at the end of the day.

Caffeine can also impair quality sleep time. It can be useful to have a 4 p.m. cut-off point with caffeine. Then, by the time you start getting ready for bed, caffeine and its effects will be trailing off in your system.

Go to sleep. Do try to minimize 'screen time' – computers, phones, laptops and tablets, or TV – in the two hours before you go to bed. There are good reasons to do this:

- They can be addictive, eating into even more sleep time.
- They stimulate your brain. Checking emails, the news and social media, watching action films or disturbing scenes at night can create worry and stress. Read a book instead!
- The 'blue' light that some devices emit can affect your internal body clock. Blue light is present in morning light so late-night gadget use can trick the body into speeding up the metabolism and making sleep more difficult. If you can't separate yourself from your phone, at least put the blue light filter on and dim the screen brightness.

Avoid eating late. If you go to bed only an hour after having eaten a meal, you may not be allowing enough time for your food to digest. Try and eat earlier or eat a lighter meal in the evening.

Create for yourself a calm, relaxing bedtime routine; it might be a warm bath or shower, soft lighting in your room. If you have worries in your mind – what you did or didn't do, what does and doesn't need doing, what might or might not happen – you might find it helpful to write them down so you can let them all go.

If you're having difficulty getting to sleep, see if listening to something on the radio, listening to music, an audio book, or a podcast distracts your mind; gives it something else to engage with. Identify and reflect on the good things in your day. Try a relaxation technique. If sleep problems persist, do get professional advice and support; talk to your doctor.

Manage social media. Social media – Twitter, Instagram, Facebook groups, WhatsApp groups – can certainly create and maintain connections with other people. But these groups can also be stressful – addictive, pressurizing, invasive, and overwhelming – and contribute to a feeling of missing out if you don't or can't keep up. Do try and limit the time you spend on social media.

Put a limit or 'do not disturb' setting on your phone. If you're waking up to answer messages during the night, you're not going to get the good night's rest you need. Be mindful, too, of accessing work emails in the evening. For some of us, dealing with work emails at home helps to keep on top of things, but there's also a very real risk of never being away from work which can create cumulative strain and stress.

Seek out nature. When First World War soldiers returned from combat, many of them were shell-shocked. Many were unable to manage home lives due to what we now know was post-traumatic stress disorder (PTSD). The benefits of being in nature have been recognized as being of enormous benefit for traumatized military personnel; veterans are encouraged to do this, to this day.

A 2019 study by the University of Exeter Medical School has found that people who spend at least 120 minutes in nature a week are significantly more likely to report good health and higher psychological wellbeing than those who don't. The study reports that it doesn't matter whether the 120 minutes were achieved in a single visit or over several shorter visits.

Try and organize your days so that you can spend time in nature. Mind has lots of tips on how to bring some benefits from nature into your life, whatever your personal situation. Go to mind.org.uk and search for 'ideas to try in nature' and 'nature and mental health overcoming barriers'.

Most people have somewhere near them, even if it's only a small park or garden. With more than 62,000 urban green spaces in Great Britain, one should never be too far away. The Wildlife Trusts www.wildlifetrusts.org have a searchable online map of their nature reserves, almost all of which have free entry; they also provide a list of accessible nature reserves. And Ordnance Survey's Greenspace – getoutside.ordnancesurvey.co .uk/greenspaces/ shows thousands of green spaces for leisure and recreation.

Spend time with animals. Time spent with a pet – a cat, dog, or other pet animal – can be calming and comforting, providing an unconditional exchange of care and love. In 2017, the University of Sussex's 'Walking society' was set up for students who miss their dogs while away at university or who, the society says 'just need some doggy love'. They bring dogs to campus so that students can join their community of dog lovers, helping to build friendships, ease loneliness, and to promote mental health. It currently has 300 members and up to 40 dogs taking part in regular meet-ups with the students. The dogs benefit from a walk and extra attention and the students find it helps their mood and mental health and that they meet like-minded friends in the group.

If you'd like to spend time with an animal but don't have your own, organizations like borrowmydoggy.com connect dog owners with others who would like to walk or dog sit and share the care of a dog. There are also opportunities to care for animals at your local RSPCA or animal sanctuary.

Meditation and mindfulness. Being present in the here and now through mindful meditation and guided visualization can help distract repetitive, troubling thoughts and relax your body. Meditations and guided visualizations work by encouraging you to be aware of your breathing and relaxing your body whilst guiding your imagination to follow a narrative that brings you to a place of calm and deeper relaxation. There are many apps available for you to choose from online. Simply Google 'Best meditation apps' to find something you'll like.

Spiritual practice. For many people, a spiritual life is to be found through their religious beliefs; the connection to a higher being, the rituals, prayers, meditations, or mantras involved. Although spirituality can be part of a religion, it can also be seen as being distinct from religion. Spirituality is a relationship with something that connects you to a purpose in life; something larger and more everlasting than yourself.

You can choose to define what that means for yourself, in whatever way feels most appropriate. People who are separated from their cultures may find that their shared spiritual beliefs and practices can provide connections with their cultural identity. Your own sense of spirituality might come from something as simple as the power of the ocean, the beauty of the sunset, or the enormity of a star-filled sky. Concepts such as beauty, music and creativity, imagination and peace, and the miracles of nature can all contribute to a sense of spirituality – to connecting with something profound, no matter how simple or awesome.

Think about what you *already* do that makes you feel connected. Perhaps it's playing a team sport, singing in a choir, gardening or being outside with nature, or being with thousands of others at a music festival. Get connected; appreciate the beauty of what we are naturally a part of, concepts such as music and art, wildlife, and the miracles of nature.

Get creative – arts, music, and dance.

Whenever illness is associated with loss of soul, the arts emerge spontaneously as remedies, soul medicine.

Pairing art and medicine stimulates the creation of a discipline through which imagination treats itself and recycles its validity back to daily living.

Professor Shaun McNiff, Expressive Therapies at Lesley University, Cambridge, MA

We all have the ability to be creative. (Some of us just haven't realized it yet!) Whether it's doodling, drawing or painting, embroidery, sculpture, cake decorating, calligraphy, origami, or one of dozens of different art and craft activities, doing something creative can be a positive way of being focused and engaged. In fact, when you are absorbed in a creative activity, you're experiencing something known as 'flow'. When you're in a state of flow, it's as if a water current is effortlessly carrying you along. Your awareness merges with what you're doing and you are completely 'in the moment'. Your thoughts are positive and in tune with what you're doing.

What art activities might you like doing? Sketching, clay modelling, scrapbooking? Know that when you need to bring together your mind, body, and environment, arts and crafts are activities where you can easily experience flow.

Listening to or playing music, singing, and dancing can also provide a sense of flow. Music, singing, and dancing can provide a focus that can range from being totally energizing, to calming and relaxing. As with art, music and dancing can be a different language to express how you feel. Sing and dance with other people or sing in the shower and dance on your own in the kitchen. Make your own music; if you don't already know how, learn to play an instrument; it's never too late!

Sex. Sex can be pleasurable, fun, exciting, intimate, loving, and if you orgasm, can fill you with feel-good hormones. There are risks attached to sex with other people if you don't take precautions to protect yourself from sexually transmitted infections (STIs). If you are concerned that you may have an STI, do go and see your GP or local sexual health clinic.

If you don't have or don't want a partner for sex, masturbation is an option and there are many products and sex toys on sale for sexual pleasure for both women and men. There may be times when your libido decreases – this can be due to age, psychological problems, stress, menopause, or illness. These times can pass. It's also OK not to want sex but it may be a problem if you are in a relationship with differing sexual appetites. You can seek support.

Laughter. As an envoy to the Church of England, Terry Waite travelled to Lebanon in the hope of securing the release of four hostages. He was himself kidnapped and held captive from 1987 to 1991. Speaking at EMDR Association's 2018 Conference in Liverpool, Terry said:

> In my darkest days, I was handcuffed to a radiator and blindfolded for 24 hours a day. I had the briefest of respite, where I was allowed to eat, and walk in the room I was held in. I had experiences of guns being held to my head, thinking (as I was told) that today would be the day I died. I was in a living hell.

Terry described how, at night, he would regularly wake up laughing, 'somehow my brain and body gave me what I needed to get through; humour! And subsequently, hope.'

Clearly, this is an extreme situation, but for all of us, in a range of situations, humour can lighten our load. Humour can often provide a different perspective on life and help see us through difficult times. Laughter can be therapy!

Do you seek out fun and laughter in difficult times? There are ways you can get it into your life. Look to spend time with the fun people in your life. Or organize a fun activity with others. Or simply start or end your day watching an episode of a sitcom (we both know two people who do this). It could mean listening to an amusing podcast.

Connection to others, family, friends, and asking for help and support. Human beings are social beings; we need to interact with others; to connect and to feel that we belong and are valued. Having relationships with other people is important; we need *positive* relationships. Who are the positive people in your life? Who do you enjoy spending time with? Who, for example, makes you laugh; is fun and lively to be with? Is there someone with whom you have shared interests? Who in your life is supportive and encouraging?

Connect with friends and family. Show interest, care, and concern. Keeping regular contact in person is good but even a message or phone call can make a difference. Of course, having good relationships with others isn't something that just happens. You have to make time and effort.

You may be someone who, for one reason or another, has moved from another country or another part of the country. It could be that friends and family have moved away. Either way, when you are physically distanced from loved ones, you can feel isolated and it can be lonely. If you don't have good friends and family around you – if you need more positive relationships in your life – start to meet new people. Think of the things you like to do, such as singing, or gardening, playing or watching a sport – and find people who share the same interests. Of course, making new friends isn't always easy. But just as keeping friends takes time and effort, so does making new friends; you need to be willing to meet others, to be yourself and give something of yourself. You *can* make new friends but you can't sit and wait for other people to come to you. You need to get out there!

Have a look at www.meetup.com. which enables people to find and join groups of other people in their local area who share each other's interests. There are groups to fit a wide range of interests and hobbies, plus others you'll never have thought of. There are book groups, art groups, film and theatre groups, and sci fi groups. Hiking and running groups, football groups, netball groups, and cycling groups ...

Mind's online service Elefriends (the name is inspired by elephants – they don't forget!) elefriends.org.uk is a supportive online community for people with mental health problems where, they say, 'you can be yourself. We all know what it's like to struggle sometimes, but now there's a safe place to listen, share and be heard.'

Do find out what other mental health support services and therapies are available locally to you. Make a list of your early warning signs (symptoms), so you can more readily spot them starting. Don't wait for a setback or decline in your mental health.

Case Study

Sometimes, being aware of what's happening to bring you down and applying some self-care is enough to make positive changes and turn things around. Sometimes the change requires support from others; friends, family and some professional help.

39-year-old Simon had been working as a veterinary nurse – a job he loved – for 15 years. He now worked for a large practice on the outskirts of town. In recent weeks, Simon had frequently been drinking in the week. He wasn't sleeping well. He'd stopped going to the gym, and dropped his weekly swim. He was working more; a colleague left 6 months ago and hadn't been replaced so Simon's hours had increased; starting work an hour earlier and often leaving up to two hours late. Although Simon found the

---

work WhatsApp group helpful for keeping in touch with colleagues and organizing shifts to be covered, he was beginning to resent that colleagues would often message late at night.

Simon was feeling tired and run down. However, he came from a family with a strong work ethic and he believed that you did not admit to feeling tired, or not go to work, even when unwell.

Simon had begun to feel anxious; he had problems concentrating and focusing at work; he couldn't switch off from worrying about what had and hadn't been done or needed doing at work. Simon's body was starting to show signs of stress and anxiety – sometimes he suffered diarrhoea, at other times he was constipated. He noticed he was having heart palpitations – especially at night – and the more aware he was, the faster his heart rate increased.

Simon decided to take control as he felt he was unravelling. He confided in a friend who suggested he should seek some help. Simon visited his GP to check out the heart palpitations and physical symptoms. The doctor believed he was experiencing anxiety and low-level depression and referred him to me (Donna Butler) for therapy.

In the first session Simon described not knowing who he was any more, that he'd lost his way, that he had, he said, 'become his work', that this was his 'only identity'. We began working together looking at past experiences of anxiety that, at the time, he hadn't recognized. Before he trained as a veterinary nurse, Simon worked in the ambulance service, which he found stressful. He eventually left and trained to work as a veterinary nurse – a job he loved.

Simon realized that amongst other things, what made him most anxious at work was saying no to others' requests and demands; he felt that if he said no, it would be met with disapproval or anger and so he simply said yes to whatever other people asked of him.

Simon wanted to be proactive in making positive changes. His work had dominated his life. He was approaching 40 and concerns about getting older were contributing to how he felt.

Simon made a personal action plan that would help him have a more balanced life. He:

- Stopped drinking alcohol during the week which meant no more hangovers and he had more energy.
- Put boundaries around his working day; if he went in early, he would go home on time. He started to say 'no' to colleagues' requests if it meant more work and stress for him.
- Left the work WhatsApp group, telling colleagues he was doing this to ensure he got a break from work but was happy to join them for social events that took place once a month.

- Used his annual leave allowance to book regular time off which gave him something to look forward to at regular intervals.
- Returned to the gym but with a less punishing schedule. He realized that he also needed to recharge his battery and not just drain it! He began Pilates and continued to practise the mindfulness meditation and breathing he'd been introduced to in the psychotherapy sessions.
- Met up with two friends he hadn't seen for a while and started seeing them more regularly.
- Recognized the need to listen to his physical and psychological 'clues' that something was wrong; to recognize when he was getting anxious.
- Learnt to be kinder to himself.
- Took back the direction of his life!

It may be that, like Simon, you are often the one to do more, give more, and feel guilty if you say no.

It's important to set and keep to boundaries of how much you do for others or accept what they demand of you. It's particularly important that you set and maintain boundaries when you are feeling anxious or low.

It may be very hard to do this at work. In Chapter 4, on pages 93–94 we explain how to maintain boundaries, assertively.

Wellness Action Plan

A Wellness Action Plan (WAP) can help you map out what needs to be in place for you to manage your mental health at work (or if you work remotely, are a lone worker).

By completing a Wellness Action Plan, you will have thought through:

- what situations at work can trigger mental health difficulties and cause you to become unwell
- what you can do for yourself to help manage your mental health
- how to manage a mental health problem at work should you be experiencing one
- what your manager and others might do to support your mental health, including what reasonable adjustments can be made.

Making a plan can reduce any concerns and anxieties that you may feel talking about managing your mental health at work and talking about it to others. By planning in advance you will know that there are things in place to support you in work.

A Wellness Action Plan is thought through and written by you, the employee, and, if appropriate, with support from a health professional. It opens up a dialogue with your manager or supervisor, in order for them to better understand your needs and experiences and ultimately better support your mental health. You only have to provide information that relates to your role and the workplace and you need to feel comfortable with the level of self-disclosure being shared. The WAP should be held confidentially. However, do be aware that confidentiality also has to have its limits. If you have a crisis and you are at risk, then considering what happens in the workplace and how your privacy is respected is part of planning. In the event of your feeling actively suicidal, your manager might have to waive confidentiality; they would have to share information with a third party, for example, crisis intervention.

You can find out more about WAPS and get a free template at Mind's website. Search for 'Guide for Employees. Wellness Action Plans'.

3. Risk Management and Crisis Planning

When you've had a mental health crisis it's important to consider what will help your recovery. As with physical illness, mental ill-health can be exhausting and can take time to recuperate from. While you are off work, you can specify who – which colleagues – you would like told about your absence, what and how much you want them to know, and whether you would like them to contact you. Think, too, how you want to be contacted whilst off work sick – by phone, letter, email, text, or face to face and how regularly.

You may be keen to return to work; work gives you purpose, structure, and time with other people. Perhaps, though, your workplace has stringent sickness/absence policies and although you're not ready to return, you worry that you may be subject to disciplinary action and your job may be under threat if you don't return sooner rather than later. If that is the case, do make sure you're clear about your company's sickness and absence policies. You can find information and guidance about your rights from Mind, Citizens Advice, and ACAS. If you belong to a union, they will have information too.

Mental Health Recovery Plan

A Mental Health Recovery Plan is a way to actively take control of your mental health so you can work towards achieving treatment and recovery goals. When, with your treatment team, you're involved in putting together your recovery plan, you can make sure it reflects what's important to you on your road to recovery.

A Mental Health Recovery Plan can include:

- Your goals: life goals, health goals, treatment and medication goals, and your overall recovery goals
- Regular activities and routines you need to do to stay well
- Words that describe you when you are feeling well and not feeling well
- Relapse triggers: events or experiences that contributed to a past setback and could do so again

- Warning signs that things are not going well
- Crisis plans for difficult times (see page 167).

A recovery plan can support your return to work. How your return is managed is important for it to go well. If there's been a long absence or you have an ongoing mental health condition, it will be helpful for you and your manager or someone from HR or occupational health to meet up and, as well as talking about any work updates that happened while you were off, discuss:

- any recommendations from your doctor
- any support and 'reasonable adjustments' you might need
- an in-house counselling service or employee assistance programme (EAP), if it's available
- a plan that works for you and your employer, for example, a phased return to work or some of your usual caseload to be allocated to others and gradually increasing how much you take back, until you are on full duties.

Managing a Crisis

Once back at work, you may, however, experience a crisis. Here we look at two potential issues – panic attacks and feeling suicidal.

Panic Attacks

Panic attacks are sudden, overwhelming intense surges of fear, panic, or anxiety. They have physical as well as emotional symptoms. Physical symptoms can include difficulty breathing, sweating profusely, trembling, a pounding heart, and chest pain. You may experience a feeling of detachment from reality or yourself during a panic attack. Panic attacks can be scary and may hit you quickly.

Whether you experience a panic attack at work, at home, or out in public, here are some strategies you can use to try to manage a panic attack. (These strategies are also helpful if, although you're not actually having a panic attack, you are nevertheless feeling particularly stressed).

Recognize that you're having a panic attack. By recognizing and acknowledging that you're having a panic attack you can remind yourself that this *is* temporary, it *will* pass, and you *will* be OK.

Focus on your breathing. Focus on taking deep breaths in through your nose and then out through your mouth. Simply breathe in for a count of 4, hold for a second, and then breathe out for a count of 4. (You could practise that, right now.) Or try the breathing techniques we recommend on pages 141–142.

Close your eyes. Some panic attacks come from triggers that overwhelm you. If you're in a busy environment with a lot of stimuli, this can feed your panic attack. Closing your eyes can block out any extra stimuli and make it easier to focus on your breathing.

Ground yourself. Focus on the physical sensations you are familiar with, like digging your feet into the ground, or feeling the texture of your jeans on your hands.

Repeat a mantra. It can give you something to grasp onto during a panic attack. Whether it's simply 'This too shall pass', or a mantra that speaks to you personally, repeat it on loop in your head until you feel the panic attack start to subside.

Following a panic attack. Your body has just had a surge of adrenalin from the fear response, so you will probably feel very tired. Remember to be kind to yourself and rest, where possible. It will help you to look back at what happened just before the attack – it may have been triggered by something you recognize, it could be an unconscious trigger.

Talk to someone you trust, tell them what they might do to help you if you have another panic attack.

Seek help from your GP.

Suicide; Crisis Intervention

What if you're so low you feel suicidal, at work or outside of work. What can you do? Who can you talk to?

Suicidal feelings can be triggered by many things, including severe depression or acute mental health episodes. It can feel like the only way out of a difficult life situation, or the way to escape from how you are feeling.

If you have a crisis plan (see page 167) then you will already know who to talk to and what to do to see you through this difficult time. If not, the following advice can help.

Talk to someone. If you're feeling like you want to die – you're feeling suicidal – it's vital to speak with someone you trust, and as soon as possible, because isolation can increase the feelings of desperation. Speaking with a friend, family member, spiritual leader, colleague, or manager at work may be the first step. Simply tell them how you are feeling. They might not know how to help but if you know what they can do, do tell them what you want from them. It may be that you ask them to get you some professional help. Please try not to be embarrassed or ashamed; you're not alone; many people experience suicidal feelings at some point in their lives.

If you are at work and have a colleague or manager you trust, tell them how you are feeling. It may be best to stay in work to help the feeling to pass. For other people it may be best to go to a safe place away from work. If not at work, go to a safe place: your bedroom, a friend's home, a library or other safe public place, for example. You may find it too difficult to speak to anyone at the moment. That's OK. But try not to spend too much time alone. Being around people can help to keep you safe, even if they don't know how you're feeling.

Distract yourself. Try to do activities you enjoy which take your mind off what you are thinking. Think about what you like doing that you can engage with and get absorbed in; reading a book, for example, or watching a film or TV, playing a video game, listening to uplifting music. Spend time with your pet.

Set small goals to focus on. You could do the laundry, make a meal, or tidy or organize something.

Write down two or three positive things about yourself and your life. It might be hard to think of these things right now, but try.

There *is* help available; if you talk to someone they can help you find the support you need to see you through this crisis. You can call the Samaritans 116 123 any time, day or night for free. Samaritans recognize that sometimes, writing down your thoughts and feelings can help you understand them better. You can email jo@samaritans.org and get a response within 24 hours.

If the suicidal thoughts and intentions do not pass, contact your GP. If you are under a Community Mental Health Team (CMHT) call your Nurse, or Community Mental Health Practitioner/care coordinator or whoever is on duty that day.

If you are actively suicidal (planning how you will take your life), access your local Mental Health Crisis Intervention team or attend your local Emergency Department (A&E) where you will be referred to the Mental Health Liaison Team. Or simply phone 999.

Remember times when you have felt low or in crisis before, remember that the feeling changed. This time will pass. Just focus on getting through – one day at a time.

Make a crisis plan or crisis box. If you don't have a crisis plan you could make one now, so you have information ready in advance, as it can be very difficult to come up with ideas when you're feeling in crisis.

You might like to ask someone to help you to make a crisis plan, such as a friend or support worker.

The UK suicide prevention charity Papyrus papyrus-uk .org say that:

> the aim of a crisis plan is to think about what support you need when you are in crisis. You could make a list of things that you could do to help yourself. You can write down the names and numbers of people who would be able to help you. You may find it helpful to include the good things in your life or things that you are looking forward to as part of the plan.
>
> There is no set way for how a crisis plan should look.

You can access their crisis plan template at papyrus-uk .org.

Papyrus and Mind both also have information and ideas about making a 'crisis box'. The idea of a crisis box is that it is filled with items that you find comforting and distracting and help you feel better. You can use it when you feel anxious, stressed, or suicidal.

You can fill it with anything positive and supportive such as:

- something to distract you, like a puzzle or colouring book
- reminders of positive things you have learnt in therapy sessions
- a copy of your crisis plan
- photographs of one or more people (and/or pets) you love and who love you.

You could also do this using an app on your phone, such as the Stay Alive app. The Stay Alive app is a suicide prevention resource with useful information and tools to help you stay safe in crisis. In addition to the resources, the app includes a safety plan, customizable reasons for living, and a LifeBox. Here you can store photos and memories that are important to you.

It's important to remember that difficult times do pass and with some preventative planning and courageous conversations, you *can* get through.

6
Supporting Staff Experiencing Mental Health Problems

It's time for every employer to recognise their responsibilities and affect change, so that the UK becomes a world leader in workplace wellbeing for all staff and in supporting people with mental health problems to thrive at work.
Lord Dennis Stevenson. Thriving at Work review

The importance of better management of staff wellbeing and mental health has been building in recognition since publication of the reviews on health and wellbeing in the workplace by Professor Dame Carol Black (2008), Dr Steve Boorman (2012), and Stevenson and Farmer (2017).

Organizations and businesses are recognizing that valued and supported staff are far more likely to deliver the best outcomes for a business. Workplaces that genuinely promote and value wellbeing and good mental health and support people with mental health problems are more likely to reduce absenteeism, improve engagement and retention of employees, increase productivity, and benefit from associated economic gains.

If employees experience mental health difficulties whilst at work, it is important that they are appropriately supported by their manager. Whether that person has an episode of depression or anxiety, they become burnt out, or they have any other mental health issue, how you, as a manager, support them can make all the difference to both the person concerned, their colleagues, and their work.

In a 2019 survey by Time to Change, 60% of participants reported that discrimination and stigma are as damaging, or can be more damaging, than the symptoms of their mental health problem and 54% of participants report that they are impacted most by such stigma in their place of work.

There is a very real need to promote a culture of openness around wellbeing and mental health.

Addressing the Stigma of Mental Ill-health

In September 2019 Deborah Lee, the Chief Executive of Gloucestershire NHS Foundation Trust, spoke in an NHS employers podcast about her experience of mental health and burnout. In the podcast (go to www.nhsemployers.org/ and search for Deborah Lee on mental health – leading the way and tackling stigma) Deborah said that she recognized her candid disclosure was an important move towards leading the way in tackling stigma associated with mental illness. Her disclosure is likely to have had a positive impact on others that listened to her speak; a clear signal that if a senior figure in the organization can talk about their mental health, so can they.

If people know their managers will be open and supportive, it reduces the stigma and unnecessary shame that comes with mental health problems. Deborah encourages leaders and senior board members to develop organizational cultures that prioritize the mental wellbeing of staff and enable open discussions of mental health saying: 'one of the responsibilities of leaders is not just to lead the organisation you are in, but to recognise you set the tone for leadership more generally.' Mental health *is* one of the 'more general' areas of leadership.

Talking About Mental Ill-health

When someone is diagnosed with a condition, they might worry about whether or not to tell their employer. Equally, an employer, manager, or colleagues may want to provide support, but worry about doing or saying the wrong thing. As a manager, you may be concerned that you'll say the wrong thing and that you'll make things worse. You might worry that you won't know how to cope with someone's response to your well-meant enquiry or expression of sympathy. But as a psychotherapist supporting staff experiencing mental health difficulties, I (Donna) have often heard the sentiment 'The worst thing is knowing someone is seeing you are distressed but they are ignoring or avoiding you, it just makes you feel more alone and ashamed.'

Talking about mental ill-health can be difficult for some of us. You may find that conversations about mental health bring up your own experience of mental health difficulties. You may have experienced being stigmatized – feeling shame and disgrace – because of other people's unsympathetic, judgemental attitude or bullying approach. It could be that in the past, family or friends suffered with mental health problems – depression or anxiety, or another mental illness – and that is contributing towards you avoiding approaching someone or finding it difficult to be empathic. It could, on the other hand, be that you just don't understand; you haven't had any experience with mental health difficulties and illness.

We can only enter situations with the experience we already have. We see the world thorough our own unique lenses with our own unique perspective. But the lenses we see through and the perspective we have *can* be widened and developed.

A kind gesture can reach a wound that only compassion can heal.

Steve Maraboli

Case Study

(Note: The person in this case study – Georgi – is transitioning from male to female. Rather than be known by the pronouns 'he' or 'she' Georgi wants to be known by the pronouns 'they', 'their', and 'them'. The following case study respects the use of Georgi's chosen pronouns.

In the English language, the word 'he' is used to refer to males and 'she' to refer to females. But some people identify as neither gender, or both. Transgender, non-binary, and gender non-conforming people are regularly called by an inappropriate pronoun; not the pronoun that the person wants to be used to refer to or describe them. This can result in the person feeling disrespected; marginalized, ignored or dismissed).

Sam worked as a general manager in the house-keeping department of a university. She was new to her role, having been promoted a few months earlier. Sam had noticed that Georgi – a new staff member – did not appear to be settling in with the team – Georgi was distant in team meetings and at times they appeared to avoid attending, by saying they had 'other jobs to do on the campus'. Sam could see that Georgi was quite anxious – on a couple of occasions Sam had found Georgi in tears about one thing or another.

It was becoming noticeable that Georgi, who, when they first started their job had a slight moustache and beard, was now presenting as clean shaven and had grown their hair. Some other members of the team were making comments regarding Georgi being 'Georgina' and that Georgi 'was a him/her'. On one occasion, a team member told Georgi 'I don't want to work with you, you weirdo, you're mental! You shouldn't be working here.' Tearful and angry, Georgi went to see Sam. Georgi disclosed that they were transitioning from male to female and although they knew that it was going to be difficult they didn't realize that people were going to be as cruel as they were. The transition was difficult enough and, they said, 'there is no going back'.

The impact of the team's behaviour was, Georgi felt, exacerbating the anxiety and depression they had recently been diagnosed with. They were concerned that if the harassment and bullying continued, their suicidal thoughts might return.

Sam was aware that Georgi was brave in initiating the first discussion, but Sam also knew that she herself had been avoiding the issue; she felt uninformed, inexperienced, and out of her depth; that the situation was beyond her life and managerial capabilities. Sam contacted the Human Resources (HR) department for guidance regarding discriminatory behaviour. She contacted their Occupational Health (OH) Department to see what advice they had and she sought information about the university's counselling services. She also looked up the university's LGBTQ and Equality, Inclusion & Diversity group, to see what they could advise re support for Georgi.

Georgi also sought HR and OH's advice and, with Sam's support, the following plan was made:

* An informal meeting to be arranged between Georgi and the team member who had said that he didn't want to work with Georgi. Although, at Georgi's request, the meeting was informal, it was to be pointed out to the team member that discriminatory and bullying behaviour is unacceptable. The team member would be advised that formal action might take place if discriminatory remarks and behaviour continued, as they constituted harassment, which is, in fact, a legal issue.
* Georgi, with Sam's help, was to make a wellbeing action plan (WAP). The WAP would specify, amongst other things, what factors at work might contribute to triggering an episode of depression and anxiety; what 'reasonable adjustments' might be made; if, how, and when Georgi could be contacted outside of work hours; Georgi's personal wellbeing resources; GP support, seeing friends, relaxing activities, interests, and hobbies outside of work; what Georgi would do if they experienced a mental health crisis.

- Georgi to decide how much information they wanted the team to know of their transitioning and what support they needed to get through this next part of the process.
- Georgi to consider joining a union, to access university counselling services, and to visit the university LGBTQ.
- Georgi and Sam to meet on a regular basis to update and review how Georgi was getting on.

Sam explored what further training she could access to help her better understand and manage group dynamics. Sam requested that she and her team attended an equality training day. (The team found the training to be valuable, not just for their relationship with Georgi, but in understanding the wider community and issues of belonging and inclusion for a team.) Sam recognized that she herself had struggled and she requested future support from her line manager.

Like Sam, you might feel that, on top of everything else your managerial role requires, dealing with staff members' interpersonal relationships and issues and their mental health is a step too far. However, as a manager, it's your responsibility to ask for support, to identify relevant training, and to make a strong case to be able to access that training. It could be training in stress awareness and support or recognizing and understanding common mental health problems. It could be training in emotional intelligence, 'courageous conversations', and/or suicide risk and intervention.

Recognition of the need for management training in mental health and wellbeing is becoming more and more apparent. In a speech at the 2019 Health and Wellbeing at Work National Conference, for example, Dame Carol Black stated: 'One area that organisations should focus more on is to equip managers with the skills needed to handle their team's mental health concerns. And this support should not be limited to line managers – senior leaders and stakeholders should also be engaged in workplace wellbeing if they are to ensure a mentally healthy workplace.'

There's a lot to take into account when it comes to managing staff who may be experiencing mental health issues. Don't let that paralyse you! No-one is expecting you to know all the answers, or to know as much as a trained mental health professional. Having some knowledge, understanding, and training in mental health will help you know when and how far you can help, when to ask for support, and when to refer someone to other agencies.

In fact, whether or not you are able to access training, this book and all the information, advice, and guidance you can read on the websites of the mental health organizations listed in pages 203–207 can go a long way to developing your knowledge, understanding, and empathy.

Planning to Help Prevent a Deterioration in Mental Health

It is important to ensure good staff wellbeing by encouraging conversations in the workplace.

NHS Employers

When a person is proactive in identifying the early warning signs of a deterioration in their mental health, when they have identified ways to prevent a relapse, ways to maintain their mental health and how to manage a crisis in their mental health, if they think these issues through and discuss them with you – their manager – it'll likely go a long way in reducing the prior fear and stigma they might have been experiencing. You have an important part to play!

It's vital for anyone with mental health difficulties to feel able to speak about how they manage their health.

Of course, a person's state of physical health and wellbeing is often easier to recognize and ask after than their emotional wellbeing. But, as the case study of Georgi and Sam illustrates, avoiding discussions can have a detrimental impact, leading to heightened stress and mental ill-health.

The earlier a manager becomes aware that a member of staff is experiencing mental ill-health, the sooner steps can be taken to prevent it becoming more serious and provide support to help them during this period.

You should not make assumptions, but signs of mental ill-health can include:

- changes in usual behaviour, mood, or how they interact with colleagues;
- changes in the standard of their work or focus on tasks;
- appearing unhappy, negative, anxious; worried about things that wouldn't usually bother them, or withdrawn and having reduced interest in tasks they previously enjoyed;
- low self-esteem and confidence; for example, they blame themselves for mistakes unnecessarily or something went wrong at work and they are unable to move on;
- complaining of being tired all the time;
- increase or decrease in weight; eating a lot more or a lot less than usual, talking obsessively about food or body image;
- increase in smoking and drinking;
- increase in sickness absence and/or turning up late to work.

Of course, not everyone who experiences mental ill-health will exhibit obvious signs. So, it is important for a manager to regularly ask team members 'how they are doing' and create an environment where staff feel able to be open and honest about how they are feeling.

For you as a manager, good practice and empathy start with courageous conversations. Being courageous means that you acknowledge your uncertainty and discomfort – you feel the fear – but you engage in conversation anyway.

It's up to the person themselves to decide who they talk with and how much information they want to share with their manager and colleagues. It may simply be on a 'need to know' basis. Confidentiality does have its limits, though, depending on the level of risk to their own and others' safety. If a staff member has a crisis and is at risk, then considering what happens in the workplace and how their privacy is respected must be part of planning.

How Should I Approach the Meeting with the Member of Staff?

It may be that someone has a mental health diagnosis and they have shared this information with you. It may be that they *haven't* told you but you are aware that one of your staff is struggling with mental health issues. Although they are not obliged to tell you their personal problems, there are some practical things you could do to help foster an atmosphere that is encouraging, open, and supportive.

Suggesting a meeting with the staff member shows willingness from you to engage and find out what they may be experiencing and struggling with, that you might be able to help with. Whether it's work, home, or health difficulties – together you can talk about what may be put into place to support them and mitigate issues that are affecting their work:

- Choose an appropriate time and place to have the discussion – private and quiet where you won't be disturbed.
- Establish how much time is available for the meeting.
- Be clear about confidentiality; ensure the staff member knows who, if anyone, you will share their information with.
- Be careful not to make assumptions about their mental health and how this impacts on their ability to work.
- Encourage the other person to talk. Listen. Really listen. Ask open questions. (Open questions ensure that the other person answers with more than just 'yes' or 'no'). But be careful not to sound like you're interrogating them.
- Let the other person explain in their own words how, for them, mental ill-health presents, what triggers a downturn in their mental health, how it impacts on their work, and what support and 'reasonable adjustments' they may need. (This information can all be part of a Wellness Action Plan. See page 185).
- Remain positive; reassure them that you want to support and help them.

Case Study

Ahmed was diagnosed with anxiety 4 years ago. When he started a job in the Human Resources department of the police force, Ahmed was aware that it involved working in an open plan office with 20 other members of staff. He was concerned about this as previous experience of open plan working resulted in him feeling vulnerable and triggered episodes of anxiety.

Ahmed met his manager Jay on the first day of his induction to the team. He told Jay that he liked working with other people but that although he liked working in a team, he was aware that he was prone to becoming socially anxious (also known as social phobia) which led to him finding it difficult to focus on his work because he felt (rightly or wrongly) that others would be watching and judging him. When he felt like this he would end up feeling sick, sweating, trembling, and having palpitations.

Ahmed had completed a Wellness Action Plan (WAP) in his last job in HR at a London hospital and had prepared a draft prior to starting his new role with the police force. As well as ways to manage any anxiety attacks that he might have, his plan identified the sorts of things that could trigger his anxiety in the first place. Ahmed's new manager, Jay, was keen to discuss his plan with him and, having learned what triggered his anxiety and what helped him feel less anxious, he identified a smaller more contained part of the open plan office where four other staff sat, for Ahmed to work. Jay further accommodated Ahmed's social anxiety by suggesting that, to begin with, Ahmed need not attend every meeting – that it might be helpful if he started by coming to smaller meetings with just a few people. Jay suggested that with larger meetings with a lot of people, a team member could brief him after the meeting instead.

Ahmed felt the WAP gave him some control; it helped him manage his mental health at work and feel relatively stable. He was particularly encouraged to know that his manager Jay had taken the WAP seriously and was open to talking about and supporting him with his mental health.

Wellness Action Plans

A Wellness Action Plan can be a helpful tool for your employee and you, their manager.

Wellness Action Plans (WAPs) were developed from Mary Ellen Copeland's Wellness Recovery Action Plan (WRAP). They have been used worldwide, by people managing their mental health. Writing out a WAP encourages a person to identify what keeps them well at work, what causes them to become unwell, and how to best manage a mental health problem at work should they be experiencing one.

A WAP is drafted by the employee, with you the manager and, if appropriate, with support from a health professional. The employee only needs to provide information that relates to their role and the workplace.

A Wellness Action Plan can help you fulfil your duties as a line manager. It can:

- help you structure and start conversations about mental health with your employees;
- help you understand your employees' experiences and needs;
- help with identifying and considering reasonable adjustments;
- help ensure employees returning to work after absence are appropriately supported.

For the employee, a Wellness Action Plan can identify:

- what helps to keep the person well;
- what resources the employee has to support themselves;
- what 'being well' is for them and what that might look like to others;
- the things that may trigger their stress, anxiety, or depression, in the workplace.

A WAP can also:

- describe what the manager may notice as an early warning sign that something is wrong for the employee;

- identify what support measures can be put into place if the employee starts to struggle with their health;
- identify whether the employee has external support in the community;
- set boundaries for how to contact the member of staff and the manager; whether phone, email, text messaging or face to face is best. Also, what issues they might be contacted about and how regular the contact may be if they are on sick leave. Be aware that too much contact might be felt as harassment and too little could be interpreted as lack of concern and not caring that they are unwell.

Plan some time to discuss the WAP and any reasonable adjustments with the other person before it's finalized and signed off. Explain what might be possible but try not to offer too much of your own advice and suggestions.

The WAP should be held confidentially and regularly reviewed by the employee and you, the manager, together.

It is vital for anyone with a mental health issue to feel that they're able to talk about how they manage their health, what the early warning signs may be for them and how to plan ahead. It is their choice as to who should know this information – they may want to adopt a 'need to know basis' regarding what and how much is shared with colleagues. However, confidentiality has to have its limits, depending on the level of risk to their own and others' safety. If a staff member has a crisis and is considered at risk, then the extent to which their privacy is respected needs to be considered in the Wellness Action Plan. In the event of a person presenting as suicidal, as their manager, you would have to share information with a third party – for example, a crisis intervention team.

You can find out more about WAPs and get a free template at Mind's website. Search for 'Guide for Line Managers. Wellness Action Plans'.

Supporting Staff Through Ill-health and Back to Work

Organizations will have policies on sickness and absence and return to work. It should be clear that each person is treated equally, whether they are absent from work due to a physical illness, or for a mental health problem. Some organizations provide for extra leave of absence to support staff who need further time off work – to see them through, for example, an episode of heightened anxiety or depression, or a relationship breakdown – without affecting sick leave.

Sometimes people feel they are out on a limb – unsupported – whilst off work sick and this can heighten the fear of returning.

When I was off work with burn out – I felt my manager was unsympathetic. His silence and lack of contact – one phone call in 7 weeks – meant I had made up many reasons why he didn't care if I came back to work at all! I convinced myself he thought I was a useless doctor, who just couldn't cope, not that I was someone who had been overloaded in my work and had burnt out because I care. I was worried to come back to work.

Jodie. Junior doctor

Being Supportive When an Employee is Off Sick

* Agree how regularly you will be in contact and by which means – phone, text, email (this may have already been agreed if they have made a WAP). Reassure them that they can contact you if they have concerns, and state between what times of the working day they can contact you and expect to get a reply.
* Respect confidentiality. Agree what information they would like shared with colleagues – others will want to know how they are getting on. Ask who they would like to hear from. Staying in touch with friends can help a person feel less isolated and also support a smooth return, so encourage work colleagues to keep in touch.
* Just as you would for someone with a physical illness, send a 'get well soon card' signed by you for the team.
* Encourage them to rest (advise them not to access work emails whilst recuperating) to get well and return to work when they are ready.

As a manager, you will need to keep in contact with HR and Occupational Health; act on their recommendations and keep people informed. Be aware that others may have had to pick up extra work. Be sure to thank them and discuss how this will be managed and how soon the work can be handed back.

If the person is concerned about difficulties or grievances with other team members, do get them addressed to help the person return to work with less difficulty.

Preparing for an Employee's Return to Work

When someone is ready to return to work, it can be helpful to meet up first. The other person may be happy to meet at work but they may prefer to meet somewhere outside of the workplace. Do offer the choice.

They need to feel you are genuinely interested in their wellbeing and that you can build trust that will help you support them in a sustainable return to their role. Be positive; focus on what they can do rather than what they can't. But don't ignore or dismiss any limitations they might have.

- Talk with the person about their period of absence; ask if there were aspects of their work that contributed to them becoming unwell. Be sensitive to the fact that they may not want to discuss this in any detail.

- Ask what, right now, might be a main concern about returning to work. Whatever it might be, work together to try to find possible solutions.
- If you don't know the answer to any of their questions reassure them you will find out the answers and *will* get back to them.
- Ask if they have any concerns about their colleagues' attitudes.
- Explain any recent changes that affect their work; their role and responsibilities.
- Have they been referred to counselling – in-house counselling services, or Employment Assisted Programmes (EAP) to support them with the transition back into work?
- Make sure that the employee is registered with a GP and let them know the company policy for allowing employees to attend appointments in work time. (Although extra time off work for appointments may be one of the 'reasonable adjustments').
- Know how you will cover their absence to attend any appointments.
- Consider the person having a workplace 'buddy', someone they get on well with, to help them reintegrate into the team. If your organization has signed up to the Time To Change pledge time-to-change .org.uk/ (see Chapter 3, page 57) they can pair up with a 'mental health champion'.
- If they haven't already done so, suggest making a Wellness Action Plan and a plan for their return to work (this might include a phased return to work). Discuss any workplace adjustments they might

need. (See pages 192–194 'Reasonable Adjustments and the Access to Work Scheme')

- Have a plan for their first day, their first week, and their first month back, with realistic objectives. Reassure them that they're not expected to hit the ground running, that it will be a gradual process of picking up their workload.

On their first day back, ensure the staff member feels welcomed and included. Do say you are pleased to see them and encourage colleagues to make sure the person feels welcome. Be aware that although the person may seem fine, they may be still feeling unwell and be anxious about returning to work. Reassure them that the nervousness they are feeling is normal. As time goes on, ensure there are regular opportunities to talk together and review what's going well and what's not going well and what, if any, further changes might be made.

Reasonable Adjustments and the Access to Work Scheme

If a person has a disability, reasonable adjustments are changes to their work and/or work environment that allow them to work safely and productively.

A person with a mental illness may be affected in such a way as to be considered, in law, disabled (Equality Act 2010). Employers must provide reasonable adjustments to people who are eligible, including people with a mental illness such as schizophrenia, bipolar disorder, or depression. Identifying the right changes at work for them now, and in the future, can reduce the impact of their health condition on their ability to work, and ensure they are getting the right support.

Any changes have to be reasonable, and the employee has to show that they are at a substantial disadvantage compared with other people because of their mental health problem. If changes are reasonable for your workplace to make, then it must make them.

The physical environment, their work routine, and workload are all aspects of a job where 'reasonable adjustments' can be made. Often the adjustments people might need are easy to implement and cost little if anything at all. For example, flexible working hours to allow for appointments with their GP or therapist. Or, if symptoms become overwhelming or threaten to trigger difficulties, to be able to leave the workplace for a break if they need some time out. It might be that a reasonable adjustment would be to work from home on some days or on a regular basis. Or, if a person is negatively affected by noise, moving to a quieter work area could be helpful.

If the help someone needs to be in work is not covered by their employer making reasonable adjustments, they may be able to get help from Access to Work. The UK Government's Access to Work scheme gov.uk/access-to-work aims to help more people with a physical or mental health disability to start or stay in work. The Access to Work Mental Health Support Service, delivered by

'Remploy' remploy.co.uk is available at no charge to any employees with depression, anxiety, stress, or other mental health issues affecting their work.

They can help provide:

- tailored work-focused mental health support for nine months;
- suitable coping strategies;
- a support plan to keep you in, or help you return to, work;
- ideas for workplace adjustments to help you fulfil your role;
- practical advice to support those with a mental health condition.

To be eligible for this service, individuals need to be in permanent or temporary employment and have a mental health condition (diagnosed or undiagnosed) that has resulted in workplace absence, or is causing difficulties to remain in work.

Building Resilience to Maintain Mental Health

In Chapters 4 and 5 there is information and advice, ideas, and suggestions for employees to help them develop and maintain their wellbeing and mental health. Employers and managers can help employees to deal with pressure in the workplace by encouraging them to follow the advice in these chapters. Managers at all levels should be reading these chapters and following this advice too!

A managerial role can be both rewarding and challenging; both in terms of meeting your organization's short and long-term goals and in terms of being supportive and compassionate with your team; to be an emotionally intelligent leader.

Sometimes it may be that whatever you do and however much you do for certain individuals, they feel you don't support them enough, develop them enough, or give them enough time. It could be that they are angry with you and with how they have been treated or managed in the past. It could be they are experiencing aspects of embitterment disorder. This is clinically described as Post Traumatic Embitterment Disorder (PTED) and can be in reaction to a severe, adverse, and negative, but not life-threatening event.

You may be trying to be a good manager by trying to please all the people all the time. You find yourself in an empathy trap. An empathy trap is often set up – sometimes unconsciously – by the other person. Whatever their problems, you respond with kindness but, for them, it's never enough. They have a metaphorical 'hole that cannot be filled'. It's not easy as a manager to get the levels and balance of support and care exactly right. You do have to be careful not to deplete yourself. It's important to look after your own health; remember, all the advice for employees in Chapters 4 and 5 does, of course, apply to you too.

However, there are often wider forces at work; sometimes, to a large extent, staff *are* already drawing on all their resources and resilience. It's not them. It's the system that's the problem.

Whilst most jobs come with a certain amount of stress and pressure, if we take, as an example, the UK's public services – the NHS, the Fire Service, Ambulance Service and the Police Force – funding and budget cuts have resulted in fewer staff and more work for those who remain. The resources and demands are such that staff feel they have to work longer hours, sometimes with less experienced staff and the strain is palpable. One nurse described this as 'Like trying to work in a role you love, with fewer colleagues and one hand tied behind your back.'

Employers, senior management, and managers have to consider if, quite honestly, their workers are in a dysfunctional, broken system.

In Chapter 3 we point out that low morale isn't difficult to spot. Pessimistic, resigned, and negative attitudes; conflict and a lack of cooperation between colleagues and/or management; little in the way of initiative, commitment, or enthusiasm from workers; a culture of criticism, complaints, blame, and resentment; covert conversations, gossip, and misinformation; high levels of sickness and absenteeism and high staff turnover are all clear signs that things aren't right.

At the time of writing, the uncertainty of Brexit has had a negative impact on business, with concerns about funding, recruitment, and exports and imports having a direct effect on local and national workplaces and employment, which has contributed to distress and concern.

Supporting the staff you do have is therefore even more vital! Becoming known as an employer that cares for staff is encouraging to those considering joining your organization but also as an incentive to the established workforce who remain loyal to your business.

More and more employers are realizing that supporting their employees' mental health is good for people and good for business. Producing, implementing, and sharing a 'mental health plan' detailing how you will tackle the work-related causes of mental health problems, and what support is available to employees experiencing poor mental health, is a positive step forward. Designing your plan with input from employees boosts buy-in, builds their commitment to supporting their own mental health and that of their colleagues, and gives you a clearer idea of the support they might need. Time to Change can help you with this. Time to Change say that, 'In order to achieve lasting, cultural change it's important to create a plan of tangible, measurable activity to address how your workplace thinks and acts about mental health'. Their Employer Action Plan is designed to be a starting point for your plans. Go to time-to-change.org .uk/ and search for Employer Action Plan.

Risk and Crisis Management

Suicide; Crisis Management

The Samaritans report that in the UK and the Republic of Ireland, there were 6859 suicides in 2018. Although thoughts of ending one's life may follow from depression or grief, they can also arise from a sudden impulsive action, or a build-up of feelings – anyone can feel suicidal.

Sometimes there are no warning signs that someone intends to kill themselves. But the World Health Organization report that several risk factors commonly act together to increase vulnerability to suicidal behaviour. The risk factors are related to social and community difficulties, relationship problems, and individual problems. Amongst the risk factors identified by WHO are the following difficulties:

- relationship breakdown
- loss or conflict
- experiences of trauma or abuse
- experiences of disaster, war, or conflict
- experiences of discrimination
- drug and alcohol misuse
- financial loss
- chronic pain
- difficulties accessing or receiving care
- isolation and lack of social support
- mental ill-health

- stigma associated with mental health, substance abuse, or suicidal behaviour which prevents people from seeking help.

As a manager, seeking mental health awareness training and reading up on mental health issues can help you to feel you are better prepared to have conversations and to deal with a member of staff who is struggling or feeling suicidal.

When – whether or not they have already been diagnosed with a mental health condition – someone exhibits early signs that something is wrong – for example, becoming more withdrawn, less motivated, and emotionally up and down – it can be a cue for you to talk with them, ask after their wellbeing and mental health.

Of course you're not a counsellor or psychotherapist, but you can show care and concern. Ask open-ended questions like: 'How do you feel about . . . ?' Don't worry about having the answers. Just listening to what someone has to say and taking it seriously can be more helpful.

What, though, if they tell you they are actually suicidal? Samaritans samaritans.org/ have clear advice – go to their website and search for 'Having a Difficult Conversation'. You will find useful questions you might ask a suicidal person, which include:

- 'Have you talked to anyone else about this?'
- 'Would you like to get some help?'
- 'Would you like me to come with you?'

Or, for someone who is reluctant to get help:

- 'Do you have someone you trust you can go to?'
- 'If it helps, you can talk to me.'

Samaritans say 'Don't be put off by a negative response and, most importantly, don't feel you have to fill a silence. Sometimes it can feel intrusive and counter-intuitive to ask someone how they feel. You'll soon be able to tell if someone is uncomfortable and doesn't want to engage with you at that level. You'll be surprised at how willing people are to listen and how, sometimes, it is exactly what somebody needs to be able to share what is going on in their mind.'

Ensure the suicidal person knows that your primary concern is that they get the immediate help they need.

If in doubt about their safety, accompany them to the crisis team. This may be at your local Emergency/Accident & Emergency department.

What happens if a member of staff is off work sick and they tell you they are actively suicidal?

- Take the same advice as above in terms of the questions you ask.
- Contact the relative/friend and GP and share your concerns – encourage them to visit the employee.
- Call the local rapid response team and tell them of your concerns.

- The police may do a 'welfare check'/'safe and well check'. Do be aware, though, that Her Majesty's Inspectorate of Constabulary and Fire & Rescue Policing and Mental Health document (2018) suggest that contacting the police should be 'the last resort, not the first port of call'.

Supporting someone in distress can be distressing in itself. The most important thing to remember is that you have done what you could and that is enough. If you're helping someone who feels suicidal, make sure you take care of yourself as well. It is important for you to reflect on how you feel and to talk through and process what has just happened, with someone you trust. If your organization has counselling services, contact them to debrief in safety. It may be it is the weekend and you have no one to speak to about this – writing down the sequence of events can be helpful to you in processing the memory of the event and can help when you have to document the experience for your records. You can call Samaritans on 116 123 at any time or email on jo@samaritans.org to talk about your experience and how you are feeling.

If other members of your work team have been affected, ensure they have the opportunity to deal with what they've experienced; advise them to speak about this (as above).

In the event that someone actually takes their own life, it is important you know that, ultimately, it is their choice and sometimes all the good will, intention, and care of others cannot change their course of action. It is tragic and sad, and your feelings will have to be worked through, for your wellbeing. Be kind and gentle with yourself.

Major Incident and Emergency Planning

A major incident can be defined as any emergency that requires the implementation of special arrangements by one or more of the Emergency Services, the NHS, or local authority. A major incident can have an impact on an organization; the services they provide, their staff, families, and wider communities.

It is important to have a coordinated, systematic plan that can be put into place in the event of a major incident. You will need to be prepared – to have planned for business continuity, how staff will be supported, both in the short term and the long term; trauma symptoms can often present a long time after an event.

Major incident planning is about preparing for the worst situation and hoping for the best outcome. Plans for a major incident occurring can be created in stages, with clear pathways and guidance for containment, support, and contingency plans for business continuity. Public services can provide guidance. Healthy London healthylondon.org, for example, have a range of downloadable guides – 'Incident Support Pathways' – that can help an organization's planning for how to handle the aftermath of a major incident.

Websites, Books, and Resources

Health and Mental Health Organizations

- Mind mind.org.uk
- The Mental Health Foundation mentalhealth.org
  .uk
- Mental Health at Work mentalhealthatwork.org
  .uk/
- Time to Change time-to-change.org.uk/
- Rethink rethink.org/
- Sane sane.org.uk
- Every Mind Matters nhs.uk/oneyou/every-mind-matters/
- Public Health England gov.uk/government/organisations/public-health-england
- National Health Service nhs.uk/
- One You nhs.uk/oneyou/#izEGKP1YX5lOPwfE.97
- Stress Management Society stress.org.uk/
- Anxiety UK anxietyuk.org.uk
- National Bullying Helpline nationalbullyinghelpline.co.uk/
- Men's Health Forum – menshealthforum.org.uk
- Music support musicsupport.org/

- Combat Stress; for veterans' mental health combat stress.org.uk/
- Cruse Bereavement Care cruse.org.uk/

Suicide Prevention

- Samaritans samaritans.org You can call the Samaritans on 116 123 any time, day or night. You can also email jo@samaritans.org and get a response within 24 hours
- Papyrus papyrus-uk.org
- Campaign Against Living Miserably (Calm) thecalmzone.net/
- National Suicide Prevention Alliance nspa.org.uk

Work and Employment Advisory Organizations

- Health and Safety Executive hse.gov.uk/
- The Advisory, Conciliation and Arbitration Service acas.org.uk
- Trades Union Congress tuc.org.uk
- Unison unison.org.uk
- The Chartered Institute of Personnel and Development cipd.co.uk
- Federation for Small Businesses fsb.org.uk
- Mind Tools – for management, leadership, and personal effectiveness skills mindtools.com/
- Personnel Today personneltoday.com
- Fit for Work fitforwork.org/
- Disability Rights disabilityrightsuk.org/

- Access to Work gov.uk/access-to-work
- Citizens Advice citizensadvice.org.uk

Mental Health Training

- Mind mind.org.uk/workplace/training-consultancy/
- Rethink Mental Illness rethink.org/aboutus/what-we-do/mental-health-training/
- Mental Health First Aid Training mhfaengland.org/
- ACAS acas.org.uk/training?articleid=2031

Therapy (see pages 209–213 for more information about therapy)

- The UK Council for Psychotherapy (UKCP) psycho therapy.org.uk/
- The British Association of Counselling and Psychotherapy (BACP) bacp.co.uk
- Welldoing welldoing.org
- Health and Care Professions Council hcpc-uk.org/

Resources

- Wellness Action Plan guide and template mind.org.uk/media/1593680/guide-to-waps.pdf
- Stress Indicator Tool hse.gov.uk/stress/standards/downloads.htm
- How to implement the Thriving at Work mental health standards at work mind.org.uk/media/

25263166/how-to-implement-the-thriving-at-work-mental-health-standards-final-guide-online .pdf

- Tackling workplace stress using the HSE Stress Management Standards tuc.org.uk/sites/default/files /tacking-workplace-stress-guide.pdf
- Supporting staff with a mental health problem mind .org.uk/media/550657/resource4.pdf
- 'Workplace health, safety and welfare: A short guide for managers' hse.gov.uk
- Mental Health and Wellbeing posters and cards mentalhealthatwork.org.uk/toolkit/posters-for-your-workplace/ mind.org.uk/search-results?q= posters
- Developing a mentoring scheme managers.org.uk
- 'Bullying and harassment at work. A guide for managers and employers' acas.org.uk
- Planning how to handle the aftermath of a major incident. Healthy London healthylondon.org
- Apps: Headspace headspace.com Stay Alive pre vent-suicide.org.uk/find-help-now/stay-alive-app/
- Guided visualization donnabutler.bandcamp.com

Books by Gill Hasson

- Emotional Intelligence: Managing Emotions to Make a Positive Impact on Your Life and Career
- Overcoming Anxiety: Reassuring Ways to Break Free from Stress and Worry and Lead a Calmer Life
- Mindfulness: Be Mindful. Live in the Moment

- The Self-Care Handbook: Connect with Yourself and Boost Your Wellbeing
- Positive Thinking: Find Happiness and Achieve Your Goals Through the Power of Positive Thought
- How To Deal With Difficult People: Smart Tactics for Overcoming the Problem People in Your Life
- Productivity: Get Motivated, Get Organised and Get Things Done

Ebooks by Gill Hasson

- Business Express: Effective mentoring: Understand the skills and techniques of a successful mentor
- Business Express: Coaching effectively: Coach others to achieve their best for themselves, your team and the organisation
- Business Express: How to communicate Change to your Team: Keep your team informed and engaged

Further Reading

- *Art as Medicine* – Shaun McNiff
- *The Body Keeps the Score* – Bessel van der Kolk
- *Counselling for Toads – A counselling adventure* – Robert de Board
- *The Gifts of Imperfection* – Brene Brown
- *On Becoming a Person* – Carl R Jung
- *The Inner World of Trauma* – Donald Kalsched
- *EMDR* – Francine Shapiro
- *Politics on the Couch* – Andrew Samuels
- *Poesis – Language of Psychology and Speech of the Soul* – Stephen K Levine

Find Out About Therapy

If you're considering therapy but not sure whether therapy could help, what type of therapy you need, or how to find a safe and effective counsellor or psychotherapist, there are two professional associations that can advise you; The UK Council for Psychotherapy (UKCP) psychotherapy.org.uk/ and The British Association of Counselling and Psychotherapy (BACP) bacp.co.uk.

The British Association of Counselling and Psychotherapy (BACP) is a professional association for members of the counselling professions in the UK. On their website they explain that:

> Therapists practise in all walks of life and all parts of society, from NHS clinics to workplaces and education. They are trained to deal with a range of situations, helping people to cope with such issues as anxiety and bereavement, relationship difficulties, sexual and racial issues, child abuse and trauma, or personal problem solving.

> We use the word 'therapy' to cover talking therapies, such as counselling, psychotherapy and coaching. Therapy offers a safe, confidential place to talk to a trained professional about your feelings and concerns. You might talk about difficult

events in your life or your relationships and emotions. Or you might have negative thoughts and behaviours that you want to change.

On their website, BACP explain how to get therapy; the different ways you may be able to access counselling or psychotherapy, depending upon your individual circumstances and the services available in your area.

There are many ways of working or 'modalities' in counselling and psychotherapy.

Below, BACP describes two of a range of different therapies:

Cognitive behavioural therapy (CBT)

CBT aims to help you change the way you think (cognitive) and what you do (behaviour). Rather than looking at past causes, it focuses on current problems and practical solutions to help you feel better now.

The way we think about situations affects the way we feel and behave. If we view a situation negatively, we may experience negative emotions and feelings which lead us to behave in an unhelpful way. Your therapist will help you identify and challenge any negative thinking so you can deal with situations better and behave in a more positive way.

CBT can be helpful for depression, anxiety, stress, phobias, obsessions, eating disorders, and managing long term conditions.

Eye movement desensitization and reprocessing (EMDR)

EMDR was developed to resolve symptoms resulting from disturbing and traumatic life experiences. It is particularly used in the treatment of post-traumatic stress disorder.

EMDR is thought to imitate the psychological state that we enter when in rapid eye movement (REM) sleep. Studies show that when in REM sleep we are able to make new associations between things very rapidly. EMDR is designed to tap into this high-speed processing mode that we all have, helping the brain to process the unresolved memories and make them less distressing.

The UK Council for Psychotherapy (UKCP) can also help you find a qualified psychotherapist. UKCP members are qualified to the highest standard; they can provide safe, expert therapy to help with emotional, social, or mental health issues such as depression, anxiety, and schizophrenia.

On their website, UKCP explain that 'psychotherapeutic counselling is a type of counselling that draws from theories and approaches used in psychotherapy. The emphasis is on the therapeutic relationship between the counsellor and the client.'

Psychotherapists may be trained in one approach or be trained as integrative arts psychotherapists, meaning that they use the arts as well as other modalities.

Below, UKCP explain what art therapy involves.

Art Therapy

Art therapy combines talking therapy with creative exploration through paint, chalk, crayons, and sometimes sculpture. Techniques might also include drama and puppetry or movement. In sand-play, for example, clients choose toys to represent people, animals, and buildings and arrange them in the controlled space of the 'theatre of the sandbox'. The art therapist is trained to have a comprehensive psychological understanding of the creative process and the emotional attributes of different art materials. In this instance, art is seen as an outer expression of our inner emotions. For example, in a painting, the inter-relationship of size, shape, line, space, texture, shade, tone, colour, and distance all reveal elements of the client's perceived reality.

Who would benefit from this type of therapy?

Art therapy can be particularly effective for clients who have difficulties expressing themselves verbally. It can be particularly useful when working with children and adolescents, as well as adults, couples, families, groups, and communities. Art therapy can also be useful for people who have experienced trauma, such as refugees, and for people with learning difficulties.

For information about a range of other therapies, how to find a therapist, training as a therapist, podcasts and blogs, news, and research, do go to the BACP and UKCP websites. UKCP can also recommend speakers.

The Health, Employee, Learning and Psychotherapy Service at Brighton and Sussex University Hospitals NHS Trust

You don't need eyes to see, you need vision.

M y (Donna) belief has always been that if you want to maintain the quality, professional compassionate care for patients, then staff should be treated with compassion.

In 1995 I started work as a staff nurse in the A&E (ED) department of the Royal Sussex County Hospital (BSUH), in Brighton. The team spirit and the patient contact were rewarding, challenging, and stressful. During my first three years there I began to notice some of my colleagues and dear friends were being impacted by the work (as I was too). Some in a cumulative way and others from particular traumatic incidents, that couldn't be 'just moved on from'. Some left, others stayed and, as I had always been interested in mental health, even in my RN training, I began to look into studying counselling. Some of this was to understand myself, my childhood, and what my ancestors had passed on to me, regarding my way of relating and living. It was also to qualify and register as a psychotherapist and be able to support the staff, so that they could continue in the jobs they enjoyed.

After qualifying in counselling from Brighton University in 2002 I developed a questionnaire and asked staff – multi-allied professional/multi-grade – (from porters to consultants) if they felt they were supported in their jobs and if they felt that access to a therapist would be of benefit to them. A stunning 98% of the staff said they believed it would.

I presented the findings to 20 of the senior doctors, nurses, and senior management.

Everyone agreed that I should go ahead to support staff, patients, and relatives in a counselling service, based in the A&E department, in a room discreetly chosen – slightly away from the bustle. I worked, providing one-to-one counselling, and also ran workshops in stress management. Another important aspect of the role was to facilitate debriefs following traumatic events on the unit.

This service was trusted and it was in great demand. One day a manager in the clinical audit department, Mark

Renshaw, contacted me. He had heard I was interested in developing the service further, as staff from other areas had asked if they too could have counselling. He said he thought the time was right and he encouraged me to approach the chief executive of the Trust, Duncan Selbie (currently chief executive of Public Health England), with a business plan for a new role/new service. At this time my interest was underpinned by the work of Dame Carol Black and Dr Steve Boorman, who were trailblazing wellbeing issues in the workplace. At this point I had also graduated from a master's programme of study, as a psychotherapist, from the Institute for Arts in Education and Therapy in London.

So, in 2009, I wrote the plan, underpinned using the premise of Black and Boorman and outlining the service I had been successfully delivering in A&E. I spoke to Duncan Selbie, saying I could see this working across the Trust. He agreed; he recognized that it made sense to have an 'in-house' service, so that staff would trust it from previous reputation and they would feel it belonged to them.

After 30 years in the NHS, I know the organization is enormous and for things to happen it can feel like a frustrating lifetime. That was not the case this time; I was asked to present to the executive team and members of the Trust board. The model I proposed made so much sense to them, described unanimously as 'a no brainer', so I suggested moving away from the EAP service (external). At that time only 65 staff used their counselling service, at a significant cost to the Trust. The services

I could provide were far-reaching and beyond the basic one-to-one sessions the EAP contract gave us.

I was to report to the Director of HR, Helen Weatherill, and Stephen Morris (Exec), who encouraged and supported me. They shared the vision that this could significantly benefit staff of BSUH. I was employed as the Lead Psychotherapist for the Health, Employee, Learning and Psychotherapy service and became part of the senior HR team.

The services started to build. The model I used had already been tried, tested, and trusted in my eight years as a counsellor in A&E.

Eleven years on I have a team of four therapists, and a service co-ordinator/administrator. We provide placements for student psychotherapists from local universities, in an honorary capacity. They describe their training as 'second to none'.

We have three/four honorary student therapists at any one time and currently have a waiting list of therapists who want a placement at the HELP service.

We provide one-to-one support for staff across two sites (and satellite services). Our services are based around:

Preventative/proactive mental health and general wellbeing
Maintaining support and health

Crisis management, including major incidents and suicide/at risk protocols.

The following services we provide come under the 'Supporting Staff in Difficult Situations' policy, of which I am the author/responsible for:

- Corporate induction proactive training & awareness of HELP/Mental health/wellbeing support
- Debriefs for teams/departments following critical incidents (7–10 days post incident)
- Stress awareness/resilience & support sessions
- Mindfulness Mondays
- Active involvement with Black, Asian, and Minority Ethnic people (BAME); NHS Workforce Race Equality Standard (WRES); Diversity and Inclusion in the Workplace (D & I); and Lesbian, Gay, Bisexual, Transgender, Queer LGBTQ+ – with the plus sign signifying other identities
- Mental health awareness training for managers, including suicide awareness and support signposting
- Major incident planning and involvement
- Hot debrief (same day support) training for senior staff/managers
- Menopause wellbeing information training.

In 2018–2019 we had an average of 65 staff referred to us for one-to-one therapy per month.

In 2018 NHS Employers online case study of our service 'Best Practice', in the same year Employee Benefits also showcased the HELP service.

In 2019 I attended the Wellbeing Conference in Birmingham, and was encouraged to realize the evaluation of wellbeing issues that Dame Carol Black reflected on – that many things have changed but that we still have a long way to go. Many of the initiatives the speakers talked about at the conference we had, in fact, provided already.

NHS Improvements (NHSi) have confirmed they are to use the HELP case study as best practice towards their Interim People Plan 2020.

I regularly speak at conferences and I was delighted to be asked to speak at a Health and Wellbeing in the Workplace Conference for Government Events, in April 2019, chaired by Dr Steve Boorman.

The service model has been a great success and in 10 years we have received thousands of referrals and numerous plaudits from grateful staff and managers.

There is a great deal of work still to do across all businesses and industries. This workplace intervention isn't just for public services. Some of these initiatives can be used wherever people are working in teams, large or small. Some of this approach can also be vital for lone workers – the isolation and remoteness of work can add to the sense of being overwhelmed when times are difficult.

The HELP service is described by staff as 'an oasis' – 'a trusted service for staff in difficult times'.

In-House Counselling and Psychotherapy Services

The 2017 Thriving at Work review recommends that organizations 'Ensure provision of tailored in-house mental health support and signposting to clinical help'.

There are clear benefits for an organization to have in-house therapeutic services for staff. The services can be wide-ranging for individual employees and will help support managers, HR, and occupational health with their work in ensuring the wellbeing and productivity of all staff.

On pages 215–220 you can read about the in-house counselling and psychotherapy service, The Health, Employee, Learning and Psychotherapy Service (HELP), at Brighton and Sussex University Hospitals NHS Trust.

If you would like to talk with Donna about setting up an in-house counselling and psychotherapy service in your organization, do contact her at donna.butler @emdruk.com or at psychotherapy.org.uk/therapist/ donna-margaret-butler/.

About the Authors

Gill Hasson has written more than 25 books on the subject of wellbeing for adults and children: books on emotional intelligence, resilience, assertiveness, happiness, and overcoming anxiety. She also delivers teaching and training for educational organizations, voluntary and business organizations, and the public sector.

Gill's particular interest and motivation is in helping people to realize their potential; to live their best life! You can contact Gill at gillhasson@btinternet.com.

Donna Butler is a registered UKCP psychotherapist and a registered EMDR practitioner working at Brighton and Sussex University Hospitals NHS Trust. She is the lead psychotherapist and manager of the Health, Employee, Learning and Psychotherapy (HELP) team. She also works in private practice seeing individuals and couples. She works for organizations providing debriefing and post-incident support and training. Donna regularly presents at national conferences.

She can be contacted via e mail; donna.butler@emdruk .com or psychotherapy.org.uk/therapist/donna-margaret -butler/.

Index

Index

Index